JN304893

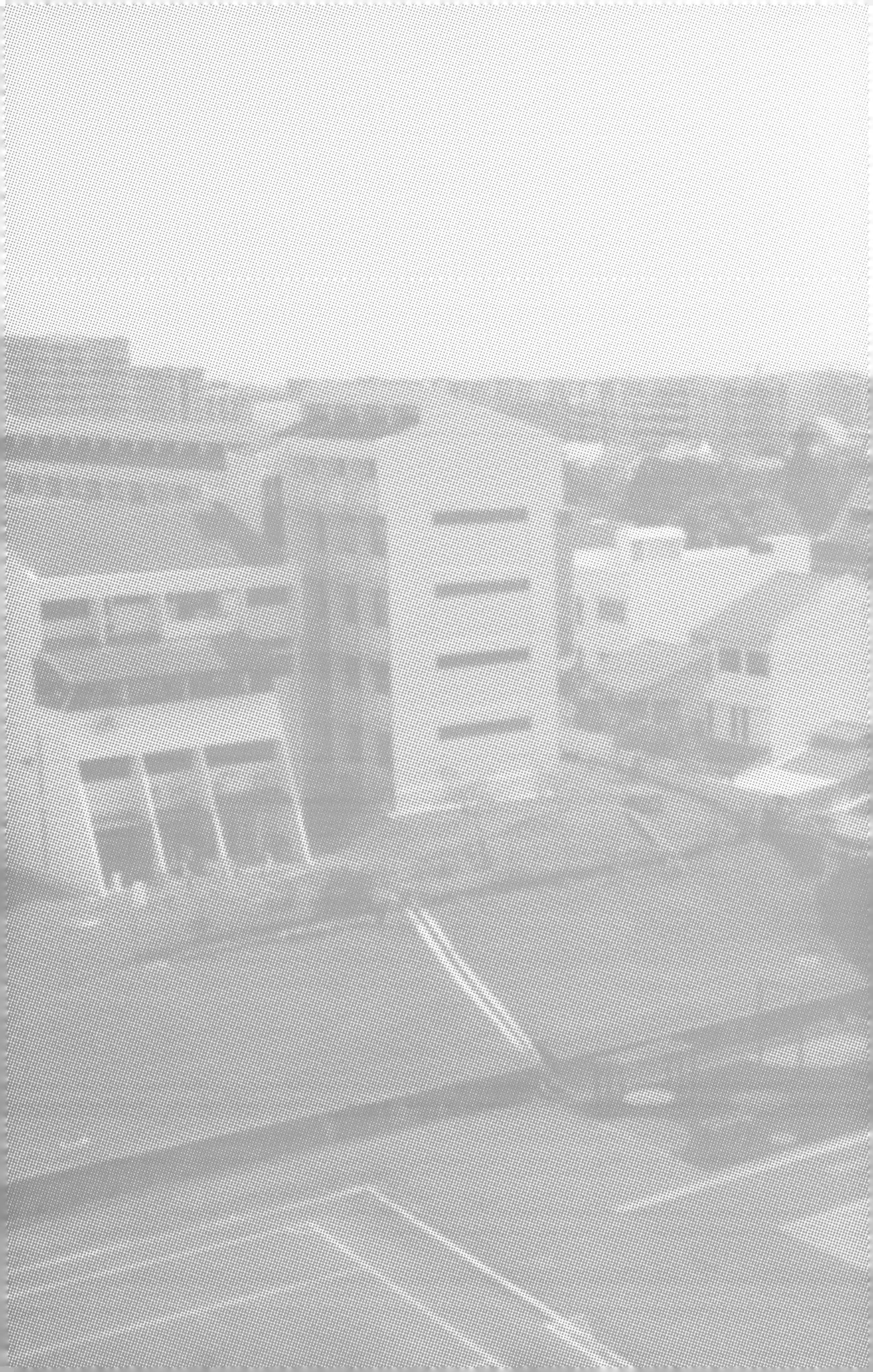

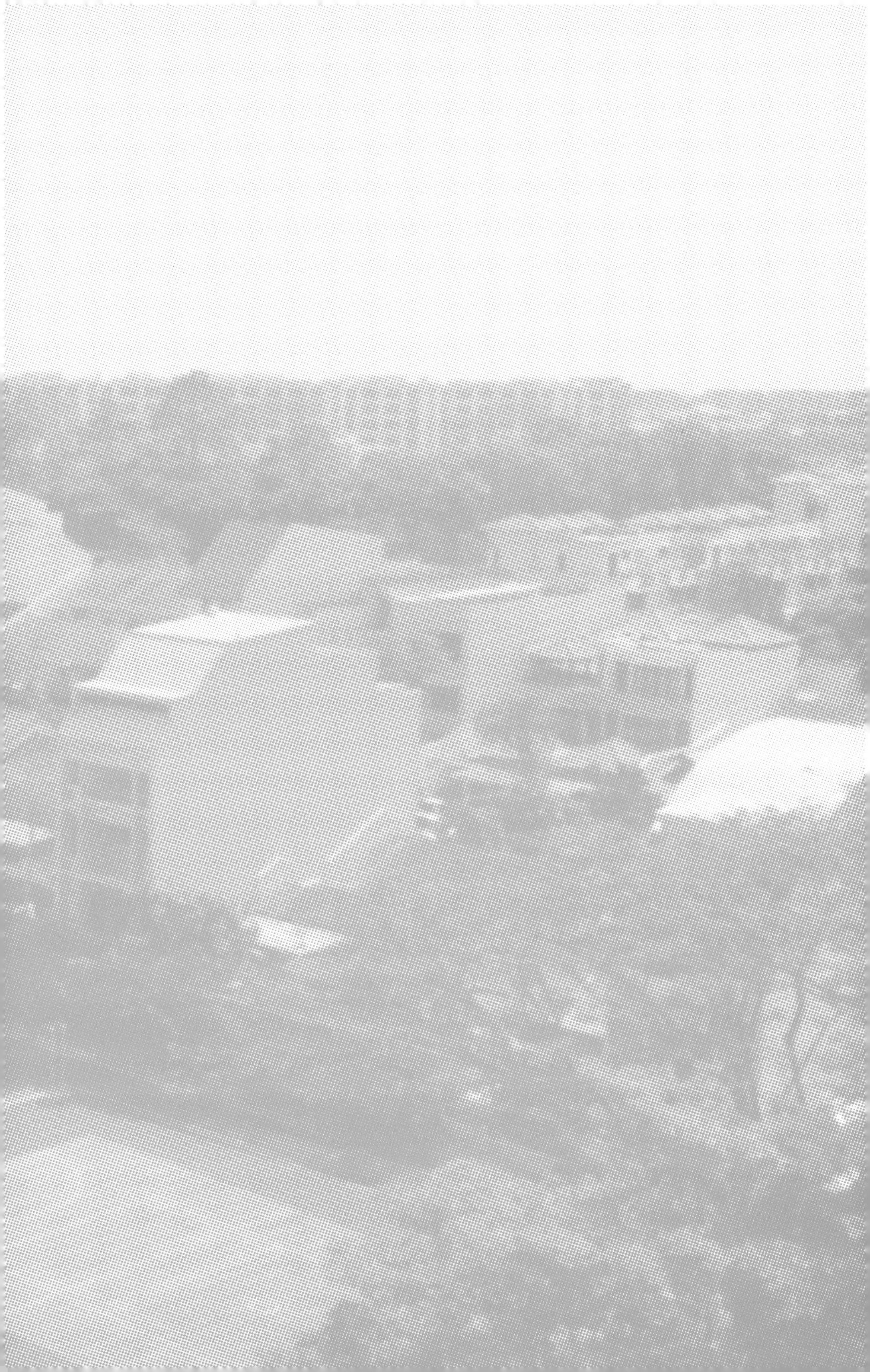

アジアの日常から――変容する世界での可能性を求めて

The Asian Everyday: Possibilities in the Shifting World

First published in Japan on October 16, 2015

Planning & Editing : TOTO Publishing
Editorial Supervision : Erwin Viray
Author: Chatpong Chuenrudeemol, Ling Hao, Vo Trong Nghia,
Maki Onishi+Yuki Hyakuda, Yang Zhao
Publisher: Toru Kato

    TOTO Publishing (TOTO LTD.)
    TOTO Nogizaka Bldg. 2F, 1-24-3 Minami-Aoyama,
    Minato-ku, Tokyo 107-0062, Japan
    [Sales] Telephone: +81-3-3402-7138
        Facsimile: +81-3-3402-7187
    [Editorial] Telephone: +81-3-3497-1010
    URL: http://www.toto.co.jp/publishing/

Book Designer: Yoshiaki Irobe, Hiroshi Homma (Irobe Design Institute, Nippon Design Center, Inc.)
Printed: Tosho Printing Co., Ltd.

Defective or damaged books may be returned for replacement.Except as permitted under copyright law, this book may not be reproduced, in whole or in part, in any form or by any means, including photocopying, scanning, digitizing, or otherwise, without prior permission. The scanning or digitizing of this book through a third party, even for personal or home use, is also strictly prohibited.
List price is indicated on cover.

ISBN978-4-88706-354-9

The Asian Everyday:

Possibilities in

the Shifting World

Contents
目次

The Asian Everyday: Possibilities in the Shifting World　　6
Erwin VIRAY
アジアの日常から──変容する世界での可能性を求めて
エルウィン・ビライ

Architect Locations　　14
主な活動拠点

Chatpong CHUENRUDEEMOL　　16
チャトポン・チェンルディーモル

LING Hao　　50
リン・ハオ

VO Trong Nghia　　84
ヴォ・チョン・ギア

Maki ONISHI+Yuki HYAKUDA　　118
大西麻貴 + 百田有希

Yang ZHAO　　152
チャオ・ヤン

Essay: Far Afield from the Ocean Current　　186
Teppei FUJIWARA
寄稿　海流から遠く放れて
藤原徹平

Credits　　205
クレジット

The Asian Everyday: Possibilities in the Shifting World.

Erwin VIRAY

Five Architects from Asia, 1. Yang ZHAO from China, 2. o+h (ONISHI Maki and HYAKUDA Yuki) from Japan, 3. LING Hao from Singapore, 4. Chatpong CHUENRUDEEMOL from Thailand, and 5. VO Trong Nghia from Vietnam, states that, "the work that we make is not in a way the definitive cross section of each country, yet there is an interest in our works to work with our surroundings, from what is possible now, and try to make something fresh and vital at the same time."

Writing a text

I am writing this text now on my hand phone. It means I have to hold the phone on my two hands, the hand phone resting on my palms I key the letters with my thumb. I assume a certain posture. What I can do is limited by the size of screen and the ability to do a cut and paste operation in editing the text. Yet as such, I am mobile, the limitation also becomes an immense possibility as I work on how to overcome the limitation. While on the train, I can continue writing, I can have the text on the cloud and then it is also accessible on my other devices, where I can do more sophisticated editing. The technology hardware and software that I have, slowly and at times drastically, changed how I work and what work I could do. This is also the same in architecture. All these disciplines are based on communication and how we communicate is controlled by the hardware we have and the rules of the software that we have to put together the basic elements we can use. Dialogue happens through Facebook, Instagram, Twitter, Line, WhatsApp, Snapchat, etc. Noticeable too is the fact that people are posting more moving images, more videos, where one has to be fast and ready to read or see what is on offer within the period that the image video is online or the chance to see it will be gone forever. It is very ephemeral. It is very fast. What I could do ten years ago is very different from what I could now do; everyday is a shifting world, changing to something new.

Human Life and Dialogue

Human life is a dialogue with the world, man asks the world and is asked by the world, and this dialogue is regulated by the way in which we define the legitimate questions that we may ask the world or the world may ask to us, and the way we can identify the relevant answers to the questions. Today, we practice our dialogue with the world primarily via the Internet - if we want to ask question, we act as Internet users. And if we want answers to the questions the world asks us, we act as content providers. In both cases, our dialogical behavior is defined by the specific rules and ways in which questions can be asked and answered within the framework of the Internet. Under the current regime in which Internet functions, these rules are defined by Google. My everyday is in many ways defined by Google.

Everyday in Asia

Each Asia is specific, so each Asia is an everyday different from other Asias and other everydays. Each of the five architects have their own Asia, and each Asia is, a context, a pursuit, a making of architecture, a definition of the role of an architect, a setting up of business, a plan, a strategy, an operation, a character building. It is a reading of a place, a city and context, and a response to that, creating something from nothing, reading a place, inside and outside, logical and rational with intuition, recognizing the existing materials and modes of construction, confronting the crisis of economic and social conditions changing drastically, plus working on themes of living harmoniously in a place with wind, water and nature and the exploration of composition and construction techniques and technologies. As vocabularies of architecture evolve each new possibilities of architecture is veiled within a little difference. Architecture and the city, dwelling and urbanity, questions to re-address the relationship between house and the city, the complexity and simplicity of: matter and space, object and void, figure and ground.

Understanding meaningful aspects of the respective countries of the architects, in the end, we realize the complexities, variety, and depth of ASIA as a whole in terms of architecture. Could this be an opportunity for imagining what may serve as best societal models of sustenance for the future? Could small things add up to something to replace stagnation with new innovation? Could this help Global sustainability? Could a lot of improvements in standard of living come not through what we normally consider as growth but through incremental technological improvements in the everyday?

The Changing World

We see the cultural trend towards the essential, the basic, the roots; The forces of economy and politics, the call for solidity in art, architecture and city planning as a reaction to the disintegration of stable states, and the rising inequality between social and economic classes. The interest in the primordial in the realm of culture, an echo of the political shift to the right, the shift towards the fundamentals in the academe and culture to the rise of political fundamentalism.

We observe the emphasis given by the architects on the elements, water, air, earth, and a reference to essentialism to the architectural discourse that is optimistic and speculative. The interest in the issue of the essential, and the concept of the elements: earth, air, water; and the experience of a person, the perception of circumstance; evoke the limits of architecture, in the difficult zone of transition that is between, what is architecture and what is not architecture. The borderline between what is fabricated and what is not, the relation between man and the non-human.

We can also recognize architecture as specific, as essential, as elements, as an approach to a new path, an alternative to the mainstream architectural discourse of binary models: city versus landscape, architecture versus nature, modern versus postmodern. The discussion of urbanism has widened horizon and opened the eyes to phenomena beyond the object. The metropolis as grand narrative of urban nature as focus of global climate change, and frequent natural disasters, where places that become popular destination of domesticated natural beauty become a place of refuge and recreation.

Nature and everyday? Architecture and everyday?

Urban and Nature, architecture and everyday: what is the meaning of these relationships? Is it to think of the relation between architecture and something else, escaping the self-referential architectural discourse, to enter into a discussion on climate change as well as common good of fresh air, with atmosphere as vital part of existence as well as our own feelings in a space? Is it to face the issue of instability, change and ephemerality that challenges traditional use of materials, discussion of the ground, the topography of the place, as well as, the materiality of constructions? This heightens our consciousness about the relation between the human body, ground and the built space. It makes us think about the gravitational forces, but also about the long time duration. The notion of water touches senses intrinsically linked to our bodies. This offer inspiration of symbolic meaning as well as functions which leads to imagination of origins of life on earth, to fluidity, transformation and expansion.

Natural elements containing the idea of totality and completeness relates back to architecture, that despite many changes that the profession has undergone, the word "architecture" has remained the same. The practice is still one that synthesizes various practices and speaks of coherence and totality, from the idea to the sketch, from the model all the way to the completed building. It will never be possible to achieve totality, but architecture's longing for order and totality guarantees the discipline a sense of place in the context of constantly changing environment.

Approaching the everyday

We see in the works of the five architects optimism. lightness, despite the heavy weight of being they are in. There is a temperament dealing with limited resources and challenging conditions. Frugality and simplicity seem to lead to learning being creative; we see resilience, reinvention, and quiet endurance. To observe other measures of growth that transcends extravagance but focused instead on the quality of life. Thinking in the specific and the essential is turning into sustainability. We see in the works of the five architects subversive actions quietly altering the built landscape and how we build the environment, not with competitively flamboyant tall towers, but with sensitivity, sensibility, intellectual rigor and great subtlety. We discover that awareness of the limits that exist, lead to boundlessly innovative means in new ways of living. We see a search for architecture that respond more about quality of life rather than quantity of stuff. Perhaps, the experience of an Asian everyday that is everyday for everyone.

An everyday that is object, yet also not an object, an everyday that is a place and a sense of place. As everyday it is specific, abounding in sensitivity and sensibility, grappling with scales and proportions, and consciousness of measures. It is an architectural operation with a concept and pursues abstraction, with relation to specific real life experience, implying a way of making through materials and methods of construction. These are responding to condition and situation, through repetition and difference, through repetition and similarity. These are happening in questioning the city and mountain, the urban and rural, going beyond categories, beyond topology and topography of a place.

Giving a pause to reflect, "The danger is in the neatness of definitions", says Samuel Beckett. So we re-think again about definition of architecture, nature and the everyday.

アジアの日常 ── 変容する世界での可能性を求めて

エルウィン・ビライ

　アジアの5人の建築家、1. チャオ・ヤン（中国）、2. o+h（大西麻貴＋百田有希）（日本）、3. リン・ハオ（シンガポール）、4. チャトポン・チュエンルディモール（タイ）、5. ヴォ・チョン・ギア（ベトナム）、は言う。「われわれがつくる作品は、それぞれの国の決定的な代表例を示すものではないが、今可能なことから、われわれを取り巻く環境と共に、何か新しく、しかも不可欠なものをつくろうという関心は、共通している。」

テキストを書くこと

　私は今この文章をスマートフォンで書いている。つまりスマートフォンをしっかり持ち、手の平に固定し、親指で文字を打つという同じ姿勢を習慣的にとっている。出来ることは、文章をカットアンドペーストするという編集作業くらいで、画面のサイズも制約になる。私は移動し、この制約をどう克服しようかと努力すると、制約はまた、無限の可能性にもなる。電車の中でも、私は書き続け、クラウドに文章を置いて、もっと複雑な編集作業の出来るほかの機器からアクセスすることも出来る。ハードウェアとソフトウェアのテクノロジーがゆっくりとしかも急激に、私のすること、出来ることを変容させた。建築においても同じことが言える。これらすべての作業は通信に基礎をおき、どう通信するかは、どんなハードウェアをもっているかに、そして使える基本的なエレメントを組み合わせたソフトウェアのルールに左右される。フェイスブック、インスタグラム、ツイッター、ライン、ワッツアップ、スナップチャットなどを通して会話がなされる。動画やビデオがより多く送受信されるようになったという事実もある。動画はつながっている間に、永久に消えてしまわないうちに、素早く読み、見なければならず、とても儚く、速い。今出来ることは、10年前に出来たこととは全く異なっている。日常が変容する世界となり、新しい何かに変わり続けている。

人間生活と対話

　人間の生活は世界との対話であり、人は世界に問いを発信し、世界は人に問いを発信する。この対話はわれわれが世界に発信し、世界がわれわれに発信するかも知れない正当な質問の範囲を限定し、またその質問に対する答を理解できるということによって、

制御されている。今日われわれは主にインターネットを通じて、世界と対話する。問いを発信したいと思えば、インターネット・ユーザーとして行動するし、世界が発する問いに答えたいと思えば、コンテンツの提供者として行動する。どちらの場合もわれわれの対話の行為はインターネットの枠内での質問や答えの特別なルールに、範囲を限定される。インターネットが機能する今の制度のもとでは、これらのルールはグーグルによって規定される。私の日常は多くの点で、グーグルに規定されているのである。

アジアの日常

　それぞれのアジアは特別であり、それぞれのアジアは他のアジアであり、他の日常とは異なるアジア、そして日常でもある。5人の建築家はそれぞれ自分のアジアをもち、それぞれ違った、コンテクスト、仕事、建築のつくり方、建築家の役割の定義、ビジネスの方法、計画、戦略、仕事のやり方、建物の性格をもっている。それはひとつの場所、都市、コンテクストを読むことであり、それに応えることである。何もないところから何かをつくり出し、場所を、内と外を、直感で論理的、合理的に読み取り、既存の材料、工法を熟知し、激烈に変化する経済的、社会的条件の危機を直視し、さらに風や、水、そして自然と調和して生きるというテーマを追求し、構成を考え、建設技術やテクノロジーを探求することでもある。建築のヴォキャブラリーが進展するに従い、それぞれの建築の新たな可能性は、ほんの少しの差異の内に隠される。建築と都市、居住性と都市性が、住宅と都市、複合性と単一性。物事と空間、物質と空隙、地と図の関係をもう一度問いかける。
　建築家たちそれぞれの国の意味深い様相を理解すると、結局、われわれは、アジアの建築的な複合性、多様性、そして深さを知ることができる。このことは、何が未来へ向けて持続性のある社会的モデルとなり得るのか、イメージするいい機会にならないだろうか？　沈滞を破る何かのための、革新的な小さなことを付け加えることにならないだろうか？　地球的なサステイナビリティを助成することにならないだろうか？　われわれが通常、成長として考えることを通してではなく、日常の日々増大する技術の改良を通して、生活水準にたくさんの改良がなされることになるのではないか？

変容する世界

　われわれは文化のトレンドが本質、基本、根源に向かっているのを見る。経済と政治の影響力、安定した状態が崩壊したことへの反動としての、芸術、建築、都市計画への堅実性への志向、そして社会的、経済的な階級間の不平等の増大。文化の領域における始原へ

の関心、右へシフトする政治の影響、政治的な根本主義の発生に呼応する、文化教育の場における根本主義へのシフト。
　われわれは水、空気、土という諸要素を、建築家が重視する姿勢を見る。そして楽観的で思弁的な論考に本質主義への関心を見る。本質の問題への関心、そして要素の概念、土、空気、水、そしてひとりの人間の経験、環境の知覚は、何が建築で、何が建築でないかの難しい境界において、建築の限界を呼び起こす。建造されるものと、建造されないものとの境界、人間と人間ではないものとの関係を呼び起こす。
　われわれはまた、特別なもの、本質的なもの、要素としての、新しい道筋へのアプローチとしての建築を見ることもできる。都市対ランドスケープ、建築対自然、モダン対ポストモダンといった、一対のモデルとしてとらえる建築論考の主流に代わるものを、見ることもできる。アーバニズムの議論は、対象を超えた諸現象へ地平を拡げ、目を開かせてきた。地球的な気候変動としばしば起きる自然災害の焦点としての、都市の自然の壮大な物語としてのメトロポリス、そこは、飼いならされた自然の美の人気の目的地になり、避難とレクレーションの場になる。

自然と日常？　建築と日常？

　都市と自然、建築と日常。これらの関係の意味とは？　自己参照的な建築論を避け、気候変動、普遍的な新鮮な空気、存在の必須の部分としての環境、空間の中での自分の感じ方、についての議論に入るために、建築と建築以外の何かとの関係について考えることだろうか？
　材料の伝統的な使い方、地盤の検討、場所の地勢、そして建設の実態に挑戦するということは、不安定、変化、短命という問題に立ち向かうということだろうか？　このことは人間の身体と地面、建設場所との関係についてのわれわれの意識を高める。それはわれわれに重力についてだけでなく、同時に長期間の耐久性について考えさせる。水に触れる感覚は、本質的にわれわれの身体につながる。このことは地球の生命の起源を想像させ、流動性、変形、そして拡張に導く機能と、象徴的な意味を提供する。

　全体性と完全性という考え方を内包する自然の要素は、建築に関係し、この職能が経験してきた多くの変化にも関わらず、"建築"という言葉は同じであり続ける。修練は今でもさまざまな修練を統合し、首尾一貫性や完全性について語る。アイディアからスケッチへ、模型から建築の完成までを。完全性に到達するのは不可能かも知れないが、秩序と完全性を目指す建築は、常に変化する環境の中で、必ず場所の感覚を鍛錬する。

日常へのアプローチ

　彼らのいる場所の重さにも関わらず、この５人の建築家の作品には楽観主義と軽さがある。限られた資源に対処し、さまざまな条件に挑戦する、ある気質がある。質素、単純性が創造性を導くように見える。回復する力、何度も創造する力、静かな忍耐力がある。浪費を超え、生活の質に焦点を定めた、成長の尺度で見ること。特別なもの、本質的なことを考えることが持続可能性に転換する。５人の建築家の作品において、われわれは建設された風景を静かに変える破壊力を、そして鋭い感受性と鋭敏な意識、知的な厳格さと大いなる繊細さで、輝かしさを競う高層タワーによってではなく、環境をつくる方法を見る。

　われわれは、制約の存在を意識することで、新しい生活様式の、無限に革新的な手段が導かれることを発見する。物質の量よりも生活の質に呼応する建築の追求を見る。おそらく、アジアの日常の経験は、すべての人の日常である。

　対象であり、対象ではない日常、場所であり、場所という意識である日常。日常は特別であり、鋭い感受性と鋭敏な意識に富み、スケールとプロポーションと寸法の意識で、しっかりと保持される。それは、材料、建設方式を通してつくり出す方法を示唆する、実生活の経験に関係する、コンセプトによる建築的操作であり、そしてその抽象性を探求する。これらは、繰り返しと差異性を通して、繰り返しと類似性を通して、条件や状況に呼応する。これらのことが、都市と山、都市と地方を問う中で、カテゴリーを超え、場所の地形と地勢を超えて、起きていることである。

　考察を中断し、"危険は定義付けのきれいさの中にある。"とサミュエル・ベケットは言う。そこでわれわれは、建築、自然、日常の定義についてもう一度考える。

Architect Locations
主な活動拠点

Yang ZHAO / Zhaoyang Architects
Dali, China
チャオ・ヤン／チャオヤン・アーキテクツ
中国、大理
p.152 〜 p.185

New Delhi
ニューデリー

Chongqing
重慶

Kathmandu
カトマンズ

Thimphu
ティンプー

Dhaka
ダッカ

Naypyidaw
ネーピドー

Hanoi
ハノイ

Vientiane
ビエンチャン

Chatpong CHUENRUDEEMOL / CHAT architects
Bangkok, Thailand
チャットポン・チュエンルディーモル／チャット・アーキテクツ
タイ、バンコク
p.16 〜 p.49

Bangkok
バンコク

Phnom Penh
プノンペン

Sri Jayawardenepura Kotte
スリ・ジャヤワルダナプラ・コッテ

Kuala Lumpur
クアラルンプール

Singapore
シンガポール

LING Hao / linghao Architects
Singapore
リン・ハオ／リンハオ・アーキテクツ
シンガポール
p.50 〜 p.83

Jakarta
ジャカルタ

Maki ONISHI+Yuki HYAKUDA ／ o+h
Tokyo, Japan
大西麻貴＋百田有希／o+h
日本、東京
p.118 〜 p.151

VO Trong Nghia / Vo Trong Nghia Architects Branch
Hanoi, Vietnam
ヴォ・チョン・ギア／ヴォ・チョン・アーキテクツ支部
ベトナム、ハノイ

VO Trong Nghia / Vo Trong Nghia Architects
Ho Chi Minh City, Vietnam
ヴォ・チョン・ギア／ヴォ・チョン・アーキテクツ
ベトナム、ホーチミンシティ

p.84 〜 p.117

チャトポン・チュエンルディーモル

EKAMAI RESIDENCE / Ekamai Neighborhood, Bangkok / 2009
エカマイの住宅／バンコク、エカマイ付近／2009

KENKOON GARDEN SHOWROOM / Thonglor Area, Bangkok / 2013
ケンクン・ガーデン・ショールーム／バンコク、ソングロー地区／2013

KITCHENETTE FURNITURE SHOWROOM / Thonglor Area, Bangkok / 2009
キチネット・ファーニチャ・ショールーム／バンコク、ソングロー地区／2009

NANDA HERITAGE HOTEL / Wisut Kasat Area, Bangkok / 2015
ナンダ・ヘリテージ・ホテルバンコク／バンコク、ウィスット・カサット地区／2015

Chatpong
CHUENRUDEEMOL

Introductory Essay / Erwin VIRAY

On facebook:
CHAT loves Bangkok in all of its beauty and its ugliness... our projects simply aim to capture its true nature.

Mission
We love Bangkok….
It is beautiful and ugly.
,,,
It struggles to maintain its own identity while trying to please others.
…our work aims to be a part of this city full of contradictions.

The exploration, definition, re-definition of boundaries; to understand, to define, to become, to see Bangkok and understand identity and how that affects making an architecture, an intervention in a city, in abstraction of the old and traditional into the new and now. The use of materials, and the assembly show a consciousness of the developments of technology to put together things. The operation to overlap the old, to clothed the old with the new and the abstract. It is a practice that is confronting the societal and cultural issues of Bangkok, its complexity and contradictions are confronted, exploring boundaries in new forms and possibilities of what architecture and design could do in an evolving world.

紹介文／エルウィン・ビライ

フエイスブックより：
チャットは、バンコクのその美と醜のすべてを愛す……われわれのプロジェクトはその真の姿をとらえることをひたすら目指す。

ミッション
われわれはバンコクを愛す……
それは美しく、そして醜い
……

それは他者を喜ばせようとする一方で、自身のアイデンティティを守ろうと格闘している……われわれの仕事は、矛盾に満ちたこの都市の一部になることを目指す。

境界の調査、定義付け、再定義。バンコクを理解し、定義し、バンコクと一体になり、バンコクを見、そしてバンコクのアイデンティティを理解すること、そのことが、建築をつくり、都市に介入し、古い伝統的なものを新しい現代のものに抽象化する時に、それらがどう影響を与えるのか。
材料を使って、ものを組立てる時、ものをひとつにする技術の開発を意識させる。古いものに新しく抽象的なものを被せる操作、それはバンコクの社会的、文化的問題に立ち向かう実践であり、その複合性と矛盾に直面しながら、新しい形態と、動き続ける世界の中で建築とデザインに何ができるかという可能性の境界を切り開く実践である。

BANGKOK
バンコク

bastard - an illegitimate offspring of mixed or ill-concieved origin.

Bangkokians seem to be suffering through a yearly dose of turmoil - from the the Yellow Shirt political Protests of 2008, to the Red Shirt protests of 2010 in response, to the Great Flood of 2011, to the Yellow Shirt Protests again in 2013. The most recent chapter in the national drama is the Military Coup of 2014, which may potentially lead to more urban instability in the years to come.

In the face of these unstable conditions, CHAT needed to adopt an open-ended architectural strategy that can absorb/synthesize such external pressures to not only survive, but *thrive* in the face of adversity and flux. We believe that to design with effectiveness and authenticity in Bangkok, it can't be just about (A)rchitecture. There are so many unpredictable conditions in Bangkok which demand that a building be so many things other than a self-referential star-chitectural icon. To survive in this city, (A)rchitecture needs to recognize, celebrate, and crossbreed with other elements of Thai life that may not be typically debated amongst architetural theorists and photographed in architetural magazines. Our projects absorb and celebrate electrical poles, dangling wires, perimeter walls, alley slums, massage parlors, sex motels, and other "inconsequential" urban elements of questionable pedigree, and happily integrate them into the architectural strategy. The result is what we call a Bangkok Bastard, an illigitimate child of architecture and ...whatever! ...that is flexible, improvisational, and wonderfully impure.

DESIGN
RESEARCH

Along with our architectual design endeavors, CHAT engages in the practice of critical architectural research.

Consequently, *Bangkok Bastards* is also an appropriate moniker to describe our research subjects. From construction worker houses to forgotten shantytowns, from illegal pop-up markets to street vendor carts, from seedy massage parlors to underground sex motels, these vernacular Bastards are hybrids of "questionable" origins, scattered thoughout the city. However, due to their illigitimate origins and lack of pedigree, these everyday street typologies are largely ignored by most Bangkokians (architects included), who simply see them as low-brow, unrefined, dirty scars in the city ... certainly unworthy of any serious investigation or research.

CHAT argues that these homegrown Bangkok typologies are infact immensely valuable. Constructed, occupied, operated by Isaan (agricultural northeast province) laborers and Myanmar / Cambodian / Laotian labor migrants, these buildings fullfill valuable social and cultural functions in facilitating the lives of the lower working class who are the true cogs of the city. Aside from their social functions, they can be appreciated for their rich architectural design stategies that creatively respond to the problems and pleasures of Bangkok life. They teach us that undesigned architecture can be compromising, flexible, improvisational, and *sanuk* (fun).

BASTARDS
バスターズ

バスタード ── 混成、あるいは不適切な妊娠から産まれた非嫡出子。

バンコクの人びとは、毎年何らかの騒乱を体験している。2008年の黄シャツ抗議行動からそれに呼応する2010年の
赤シャツ抗議行動、2011年の大洪水、そして再び2013年の黄シャツ抗議行動。
直近の2014年の軍事クーデターによる国家的な事件は今後、ますます都市の不安定を引き起こしかねない。
これらの不安定要素に直面し、チャットが、災害や変動の中を生き残るだけでなく、成長するためには、
こうした外的プレッシャーを吸収し、統合できるような、幅広い建築的戦略を採用する必要があった。
バンコクで実践的に、確実に、デザインするということは、大文字の建築に関わるというだけでは足りないと、われわれは
信じている。バンコクには予測不能な条件があまりにも多く、ひとつの建物に求められるのは、自己証明的、
スター建築家的アイコンではなく、もっとたくさんのことである。
この都市で生き残るために、大文字の建築に求められているのは、建築雑誌に写真を撮られることとか、
建築理論家たちにありがちな議論をすることなどではなく、タイの生活を認識し、祝福し、それをほかの要素と
交配させることである。われわれのプロジェクトでは、電柱や垂れ下がる電線、周壁やスラムの路地、マッサージパーラーや
セックスモーテル、そのほか"取るに足りない"怪しい由来の都市の構成物を飲み込んで、祝福し、
それらを建築的戦略の中に楽しく統合する。
その結果がいわゆる、バンコク・バスタード、建築の非嫡出子……
そのほか呼び名は何でもいいのだが！　柔軟で、即興的で素晴らしく不純なものである。

デザインリサーチ

建築のデザインへの取り組みと同時にチャットは批評的な建築リサーチを行っている。

もちろん、バンコク・バスタードはわれわれのリサーチ課題を適切に表現する渾名でもある。建設労働者の家から忘れられたスラムまで、
非合法のポップアップ・マーケットから路上の屋台まで、貧相なマッサージパーラーからアングラのセックスモーテルまで、これらヴァナキュラーな
バスターズは、都市中にばらまかれた由来の"怪しい"混合物である。しかし、それは不純で私生児的な起源と"正統性"の欠落のためではあるが、
これら路上の日常的なタイポロジーは、バンコク市民（建築家も含め）からはほとんど無視され、低級で洗練しない、都市の汚点として、
真面目に調査したり、研究したりするに値しないものと、間違いなく思われている。

これら自前のバンコクのタイポロジーが実際は、限りなく価値のあるものであると、チャットは考えている。
イーサーン（農業中心のタイ東北部）からの労働者や、ミャンマー、カンボジア、ラオスからの移民が建て、住み、使う、これらの建築物は、
都市にとって歯車の歯でしかない下層労働者の生活の手助けをするのに、社会的、文化的に重要な役割を果たしている。社会的な役割を別にしても、
それらはまた、バンコク・ライフの問題や楽しみをこんなにも創造的に解決する、豊かな建築デザインの戦略でもあるという点で価値がある。
デザインされていない建築が、妥協を許し、柔軟で即興的で、サヌック（楽しみ）でもあり得るということを、それらは教えてくれるのである。

EKAMAI RESIDENCE ekamai neighborhood, bangkok, 2009
エカマイの住宅 エカマ コク、2009

CONSTRUCTION WORKER HOUSE, bangkok, 2014
建設労働者の住宅、バンコク、2014

Construction workers in Thailand live right on the construction site in makeshift houses that fill the gaps between the building under constructing and the site boundary. The structures shift / adapt to changing conditions of the jobsite and consist of an internal core of sleeping rooms and an outdoor multi-purpose scaffolding that serves as circulation and "veranda" living room.

タイの建設労働者は、まさに現場の建設中の建物と敷地境界の隙間に建てた仮設住宅に住む。構造は現場の状況によって順応し変化する。内部のコアが寝る場所で、アウトドアの多目的な足場組みが、サーキュレーションと"ベランダ"リビングになる。

"third space" scaffolding
"第3の空間"の足場組み

building core
ビルディング・コア

This worker house is
pushed right up to a high
speed road. Life on the
"scaffolding" verandah is
advertised like a surreal
living billboard that enliv-
ens the street.

労働者住宅は高速道路に
めり込んで建ち上げられた。
足場組みのベランダの日常が
生きているシュールな
看板のように、街路を活気付ける。

construction worker house along freeway, rama 9 area
高速道路沿いの労働者住宅、ラーマ9地区

The Ekamai House is a new perimeter wall house typology that re-establishes the lost connections between public and private realms in Bangkok without sacrificing security and privacy for the inhabitants inside the property. Whereas before, the perimeter street wall and the residence were two separate entities in the typical Bangkok suburban home, they now become one hybrid architecture in the Ekamai House. The operable wooden shutters that line the perimeter wall can be opened when the owners want to reconnect with the city ...whether chatting with neighbors, buying snacks from vendors, or just watching life go by in the neighborhood. The openings also allow breezes to enter the garden and the house for much needed ventilation. Boundaries between house, garden, and street become blurred, and city life flows freely. At night, the panels can be closed and securely locked, to protect the inhabitants from perils of the city.

diagram of neighborhood street as community "room"
コミュニティの"部屋"としての近隣街路のダイアグラム

neighbors
隣人たち

canal-side construction worker house, rama 9 area
運河沿いの労働者住宅、ラーマ9地区

waterside living:
This worker house occupies a narrrow gap between the highrise under construction and a klong (canal) in the back of the site.

水辺のリビング:
この労働者住宅は建設中の高層ビルとクーロン（運河）の間の狭いギャップを占拠している。

24

「エカマイの住宅」は、住人のセキュリティとプライバシーを犠牲にせず、バンコクの失われた公的領域と私的領域の結び付きを再生させる、新しい周壁住宅である。バンコク郊外の典型的な住宅では、街路側の周壁と住宅本体はふたつの別の存在だったが、ここではひとつのハイブリッド建築になった。周壁の木製可動シャッターはオーナーが街と繋がりたい時、……隣人とお喋りしたり、物売りから何か買ったり、あるいはただ近隣の人たちの行き交いを眺めたい時、開けることができる。この開口からは風が、換気が必要な庭や家の中に入ってくる。家、庭、街路の境界が不鮮明にされ、都市の生活が自由に入り込んでくる。夜にはパネルは閉じ、しっかり施錠され、都市の危険から住人を守る。

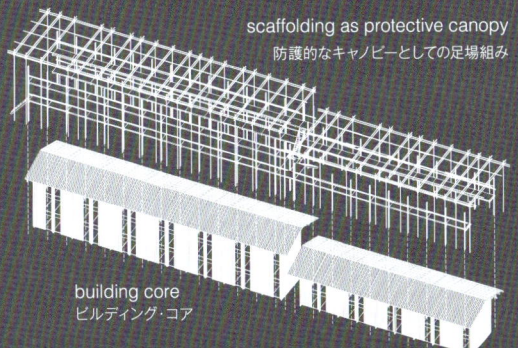

street view, perimeter wall open
通りから開いている周壁を見る

scaffolding as protective canopy
防護的なキャノピーとしての足場組み

building core
ビルディング・コア

scaffolding as protective canopy:
Here, the scaffolding veranda beomes a waterfront balcony for breezy living. The structure also supports a double roof that protects the house from falling construction debris.

防護的なキャノピーとしての足場組み
ここでは足場組みのベランダが、水辺のバルコニーになって、リビングに風が通る。
足場組みの構造は、落下する工事中のくずから防護する、2重の屋根も支える。

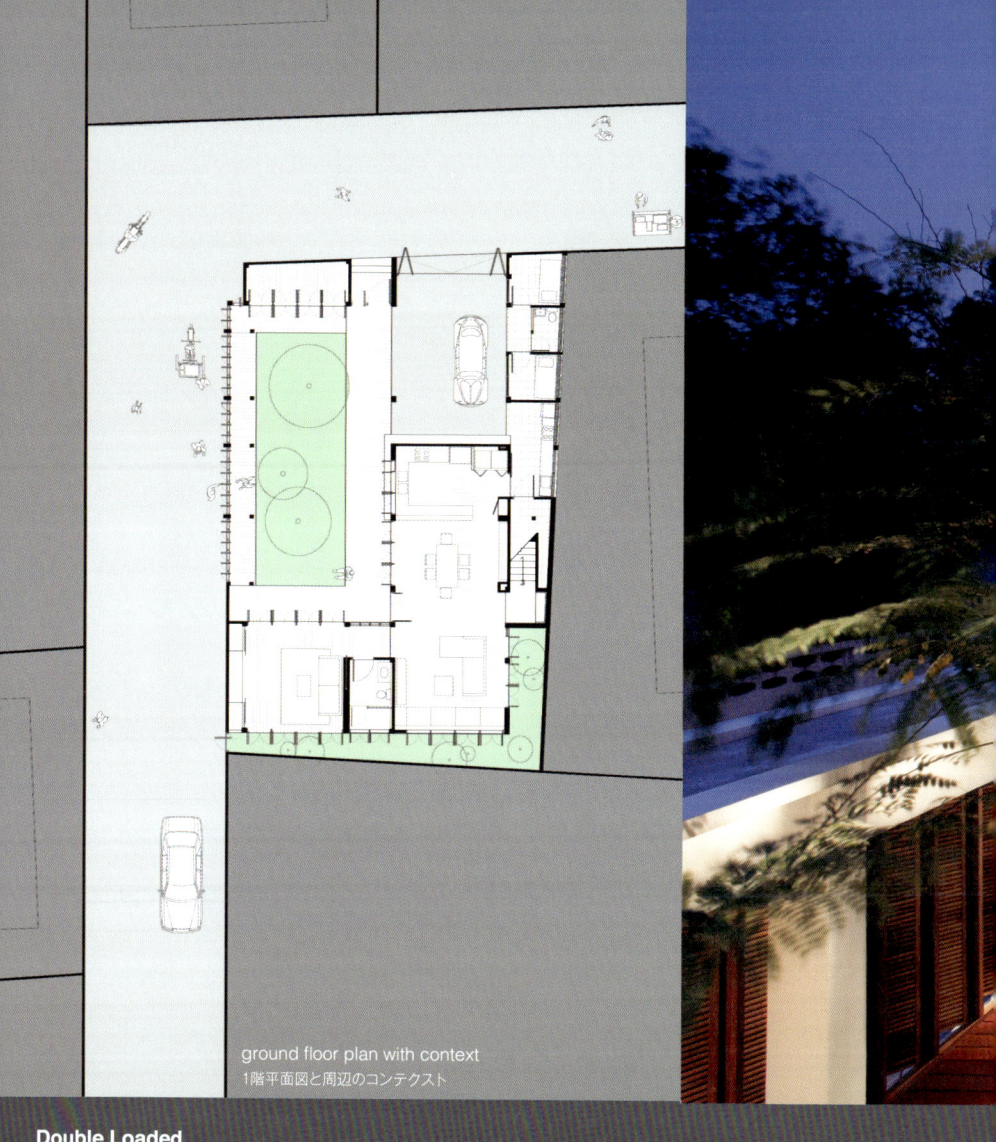

ground floor plan with context
1階平面図と周辺のコンテクスト

Double Loaded Scaffolding.
The scaffolding becomes a ventilated double-loaded "living" corridor.

2段の足場組み
足場組みは換気された段組の"リビング"コリドールとなる。

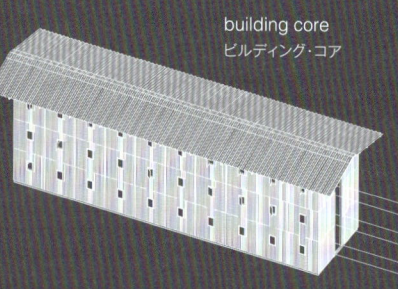

building core
ビルディング・コア

"third space" scaffolding as double loaded corridor
2段組のコリドールとしての"第3の空間"の足場組み

view of courtyard
コートヤードを見る

Double Loaded Type.
The circulation veranda occupies an open air gap in the middle of the structure. The 3-storey circulation spine acts as a ventilated communal living space for all the inhabitants.

段組のタイプ
構造体の真ん中の外に開いたギャップが、サーキュレーション用のベランダになっている。層のサーキュレーションの背骨部分が、全住人の共用の換気されたリビングスペースとして機能する。

construction worker house, on nuch area
労働者住宅、ヌック地区

view of interior out to courtyard
内部からコートヤードを見る

"veranda" scaffolding serves as circulation and open for lounging, cooking, eating, washing, hanging, napping, socializing, and drinking.

"ベランダ" 足場組みは、サーキュレーション空間であり、休憩、料理、飲食、洗濯、物干、まどろみ、社交空間として機能する。

"double-loaded" scaffolding is created when two houses are pushed together. Breezes can still pass through the corridor to provide for ventilated, shaded living.

"2段の" 足場組みは、2軒の家がくっついた時に生まれる。風が通り抜け、換気され日陰をつくるリビングとなる。

28

view through peremeter wall out to street life
周壁から街路の人の行き交いを見る

In-house Bar-B-Q stand / grocery store occuping one of the rental rooms, serves as alternative food source for the workers.

労働者住宅内のバーベキュースタンド兼食料品店は、賃貸住宅のひとつにあり、労働者のためのもうひとつの食料供給源である。

Informal transporatation network: Ride sharing back to rural areas or trucks to assist in moving are only a celphone call away.

非公式の輸送ネットワーク：地方へ帰る車の相乗りや移動手段のトラックは、携帯で呼ぶ。

KENKOON GARDEN SHOWROOM thonglor area, bangkok, 2013
ケンクン・ガーデン・ショールーム、バンコク・ソングロー地区、2013

MOBILE POP-UP MARKETS, bangkok, 2014
モバイル・ポップアップ・マーケット、バンコク、2014

Expandable pick-up pop-up market:
Pick-up truck vendors supply necessary daily products to construction worker communities. They roam the city in search of construction sites, setting up a "pop-up" sidewalk market within minutes to supply their wares. Just as quickly, they can pack up in an instant when the police arrrive to chase them away.

拡張可能なピックアップ、ポップアップ・マーケット：
ピックアップ・トラックの物売りが建設労働者のコミュニティに日用品を売りに来る。彼らは建設現場を求めて街を動き回り、瞬時に道端で"ポップアップ"マーケットを立ち上げる。警官が来るとこれまた瞬時に畳んでしまう。

view of pop-up market elevation on sidewalk
側道の「ポップアップ・マーケット」を見る

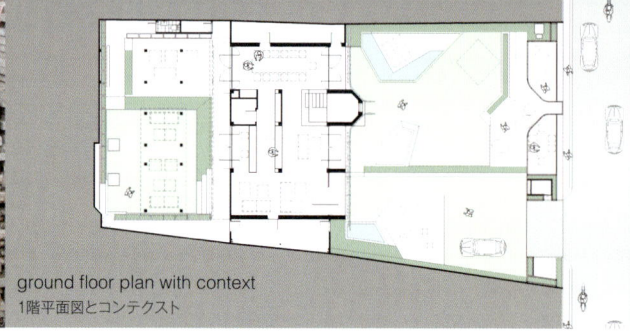

discarded wood for Kenkoon factory
ケンクン工場の廃棄木材

ground floor plan with context
1階平面図とコンテクスト

The Kenkoon Showroom is set in an existing 70's Modern Tropical home situated in a tropical garden. Recycled materials of teak wood strips and stainless steel tubes, the very materials used to construct the company's signature outdoor furniture, are utilized to transform the former residence into a new garden showroom for the city.

Teak wood strips salvaged from old broken chairs are woven together to create a faceted tropical "blouse" to lightly veil the old building, yet allowing its iconic stair core to peek through. An outdoor "sidewalk gallery" of glass and reflective stainless steel tubes display furniture pieces in a surreal roadside "living room" straddled between the private tropical garden and busy street. The dual transparency and reflectivity of the thick boundary zone collapse the two worlds, creating a new Bangkok perimeter wall typology.

「ケンクン・ショールーム」は既存の熱帯庭園内にある1970年代モダン熱帯住宅内につくられた。
住宅を都市のガーデン・ショールームに変換するのに、ケンクン社の看板商品のアウトドア家具の
チーク材とステンレス管を、リサイクルして利用した。

古い壊れた椅子から回収したチークの板材を寄せ合わせて、古い建物の表面に熱帯の"ブラウス"のようにまとわせた。
それでもアイコンである段々の芯が垣間見える。ガラスと光沢面のステンレス管で出来た、アウトドア"歩道ギャラリー"には
家具が展示され、プライベートの熱帯ガーデンと活気のある通りとの間に跨がる、シュールな道端のリビングルームになっている。
厚い境界ゾーンの透明、反射の二面性が、ふたつの世界を崩壊させ、新しいバンコクの周壁のタイポロジーをつくる。

view of pop-up market in freeway context
高速道路のコンテクストの中の「ポップアップ・マーケット」

view from entry court

view through sidewalk gallery out to street
側道ギャラリーを通して通りを見る

plan of pop-up market in freeway context
高速道路のコンテクストの中の「ポップアップ・マーケット」平面図

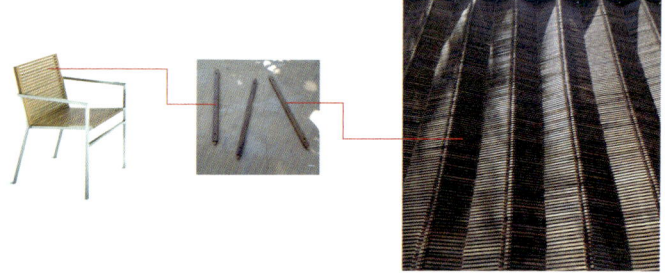

facade of recycled slats from old chairs
椅子からリサイクルした細片のファサード

Compact Pick-up Convenience Store:
Pick-up truck vendors also come in the form of compact store-on-wheels, utilizing every surface of the rear bed to display products of everyday use.

コンパクト・ピックアップ・コンビニエンス・ストア：
ピックアップ・トラックの物売りは荷台一杯に日用品をディスプレイしている。

view of wood of recycled facade from garden
リサイクルした細片のファサードをガーデン側から見る

Moto-market:
with customized rear seat armature, vendors can transform their motorcycles into a mini-market that roam the streets for seekers of fresh produce.

モト・マーケット:
特製のリアシート上の骨組みに転換して、新鮮な品を求める人のために、街を売り歩く。

KITCHENETTE FURNITURE SHOWROOM
thonglor area, bangkok, 2009, in collaboraton with b/A/R
キチネット・ファーニチャ・ショールーム バンコク・ソングロー地区、2009、b/A/Rとの協働

PALETTE FURNITURE MARKET, klong toey, bangkok, 2014
パレット・ファニチャー・マーケット、バンコク、クロントゥーイ、2014

Slum dwellers living next to Thailand Port Authority collect discarded shipping palettes to create finely crafted furniture. Their live/work workshops occupy a 2-meter wide slither of land between the railroad tracks and a freeway. They skillfully arrange their cramped space to accommodate workshop, showroom, storage, and living. The sidewalk becomes their furniture showroom for passing motorists.

タイ国港湾局に隣接するスラムの住人は、廃棄されたフォークリフト用パレットを、木工家具を作るために集める。彼らの職住の工房は、鉄道と高速道路の間の滑り落ちそうな幅2mの場所にある。彼らはうまい具合に狭小の空間をアレンジして工房、ショールーム、倉庫、そして住まいにしている。
歩道は通過するモータリスト向けの家具のショールームになる。

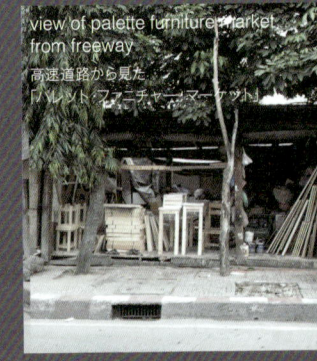

view of palette furniture market from freeway
高速道路から見た
「パレット・ファニチャー・マーケット」

37

The Kitchenette Furniture Showroom sits in a long, narrow site fronted by a large concrete transformer structure and dangling electrical wires. But instead of blocking these "ugly" city elements out, the project accepts that street infrastructure is a part of Bangkok life and adopts the architectural DNA of the electrical poles. Thus, the structure is conceived more as an open-frame urban infrastructure rather than an architectural "building". The bare concrete frame defines an internal "soi", or alley, that not only creates additional shopfronts for the owners, but divert sidewalk traffic into the vertical garden located at center of the building...thus creating a new public space for the city.

「キチネット・ファニチャー・ショールーム」は、大きなコンクリート製の変圧器と垂れ下がる電線に面する、狭く長い奥行きの敷地にある。"醜悪な"都市の構成物を拒否する代わりに、このプロジェクトでは、これら街路のインフラをバンコクの都市生活の一部として受け入れ、電柱の建築的DNAを応用した。こうして構造体は"建築物"というよりも、オープンなフレームの都市のインフラとして考えられている。剥き出しのコンクリートのフレームが、内部の"ソイ"路地を縁取り、オーナーのためにショップフロントを付加するだけでなく、側道の人の流れを脇にそらし、建物の中心にあるヴァーティカル・ガーデンへと引っ張る……こうして新しい公共空間をつくり出している。

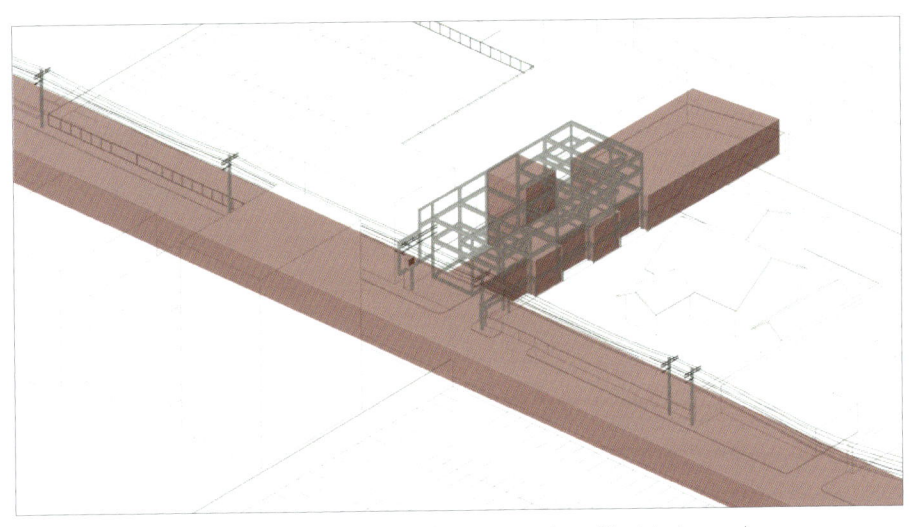

The building is conceived as an urban infratructural frame... extensions of the telephone poles.
The public street (red mass) is allowed to penetrate into the frame becoming alley extensions.
この建築は都市のインフラのフレームとして捉えられる……電話柱の延伸。
公共の街路はフレームの中へ侵入し、路地の延長となる。

Freeway Side:
The sidewalk becomes a furniture showroom for passing motorists. It is also a spillout workspace to dismantle and prepare the pallettes into clean wood planks for furniture crafting.

高速道路の横:
歩道は通過するモータリスト向けの家具のショールームになる。ここにはパレットを分解し、家具のためのきれいな木材をつくるための工房もはみ出ている。

sidewalk showroom
側道のショールーム

recycling palettes
リサイクルされるパレット

Railroad Side:
The railroad track alley behind become open-air workshop zone, which can be quickly dismantled and moved when daily trains pass through.

鉄道の横:
背後の鉄道の軌道は戸外の工房になる。列車が通る時には、片付けられ、素早く移動する。

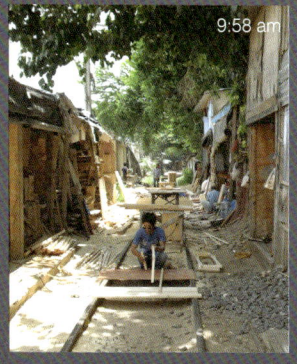

9:58 am

10:00 am

#	
1	rice paddy
2	transformer room
3	vertical garden room
4	vine room
5	studio 1
6	studio 2
7	studio 3
8	studio 4
9	studio 5
10	studio 6
11	studio 7
12	orchid mezzanine
13	roof garden
14	stair well
15	office

section as collage of bangkok textures
断面図、バンコクのテクスチャーのコラージュ

aerial photo of pallette furniture market strip - 500 meters long, 2 meters wide
「パレット・ファニチャー・マーケット」の航空写真－500mの長さ、2m幅

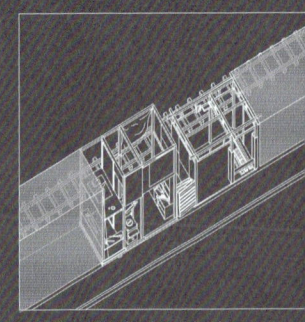

workshop / loft with skipping secton
ワークショップ／ロフト　スキップフロア断面

40

rear parking court as pocket park for shophouse neighbors
後ろのパーキング・コートはショップハウスの人びとのポケットパーク

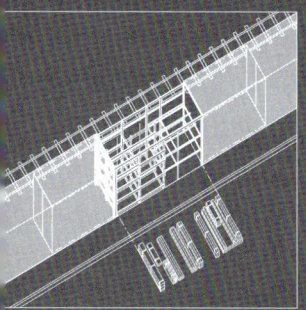

imber storage wall
木製倉庫の壁

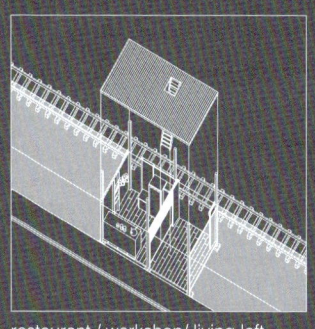

restaurant / workshop/ living loft
レストラン／ワークショップ／リビングロフト

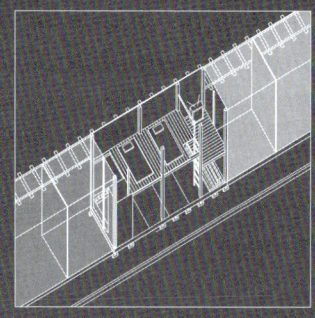

workshop / loft with loop section
ワークショップ／ロフト　ループ断面

NANDA HERITAGE HOTEL, wisut kasat area, bangkok, 2015, in collaboraton with b/A/R
ナンダ・ヘリテージ・ホテルバンコク　ウィスット・カサット地区、2015、b/A/Rと協働

CURTAIN SEX MOTEL, bangkok, recorded 2012-2015
カーテン・セックス・モーテル、バンコク、2012-2015

The curtain sex motel is a mysterious building type in Bangkok that serves the Thai's secret lifestyle. Unfaithful husbands head to this motel for a secret rendezvous with their mistresses. The urban condition and architecture of each motel is carefully considered and orchestrated to accomodate the secret behavior of the patrons.

「カーテン・セックス・モーテル」は、タイの秘密の生活を支える、バンコクの神秘的なビルディング・タイプである。不実な夫が愛人とこのモーテルで密会する。モーテルの都市的条件と建築が、利用者の秘密の行為を注意深く包み込む。

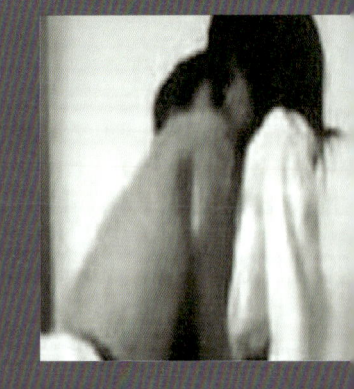

Curtain Motel District, Wisut Kasat Neighborhood
The Wisut Kasat Neighborhood at the edge of Old Bangkok was once reknown as the red light district for local Thai men. Gentlemen, young and old, would bring their girlfriends / mistresses / escorts to the many curtain motels that can be found in this area. They are strung along Wisut Kasat Road, engulfed in a dense urban fabric of the block.

カーテン・モーテル地区、ウィスット・カサット地区
バンコクの旧市街の端部にあるウィスット・カサット地区は、かつてタイの男の赤灯地区として知られていた。老若の紳士が恋人や愛人をエスコートしたカーテン・モーテルがこの地域にはたくさんあり、ウィスット・カサット通りに伸び、高密度のブロックの中に飲み込まれている。

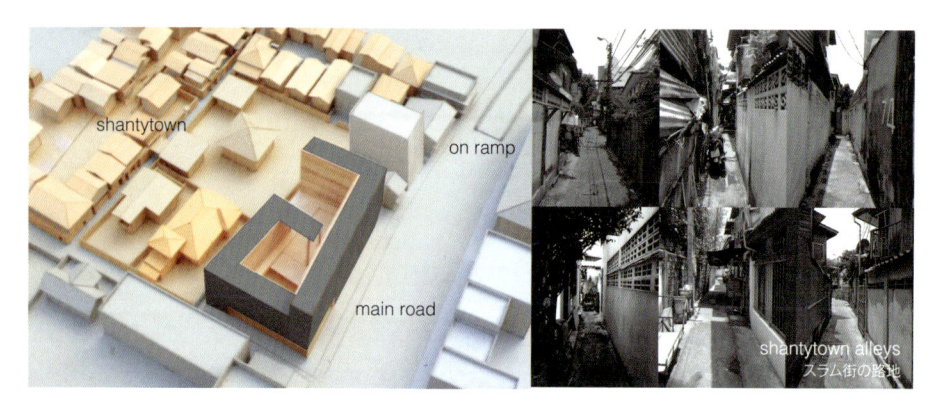

The Nanda Heritage Hotel is situated between two worlds. In front the building faces a high-speed onramp to a major river bridge. In back, it is surrounded by a 100-year-old maze-like Purinayok shantytown. The dark outside shell, a simple concrete frame with brick infill, contains the guest rooms. This perimeter mass responds to differing urban conditions through the manipulation of scale and linear drip edge details. At the same time, it also protects a hidden inner open-air courtyard of a completely different tectonic. This inner core is a light steel scaffolding that delicatley suspends "found" elements salvaged from the owners' 1912 family teak wood mansion. Old doors, windows, floor boards, wall panels, handrails, and stairs…all of aged vintage teak wood... create an inner sanctuary that integrate "found" materials with new construction components. It is a lesson learned come from the ingenuity of our local shanty neighbors, who make beautiful spaces through a makeshift compositions of found objects. Furthermore, the inner courtyard is a spatial extention of the labyrinthian alley network of the shantytown …but attempts to translate the mazelike circulation from *plan* into *section*.

「ナンダ・ヘリテージ・ホテル」はふたつの世界の間にある。前面は大きな河の橋に向かう高速の入り口に面し、背面は100年前から続く迷路のようなプリナヨクのスラム街に面している。暗色の外殻、インフィルに煉瓦を使った、シンプルなコンクリートのフレームの中に客室がある。この外周面のマッスは、スケールや端部から滴るディテールの操作を通して、異なる都市の状況に呼応している。同時に、全く異なる工法の内に隠れたコートヤードを守ってもいる。この内なるコアは、オーナー家族の1912年のチーク材のマンションから回収された"発見された"部材が繊細に使用されている。古いドア、窓、床材、壁パネル、手摺、階段……すべて年を経たチーク材……が"発見された"材料を総合し、新しい建築材料で包んだ、内なる聖域がつくられた。見つけてきたものをやりくりして、美しい空間をつくる、スラムの住人の発明の才から学んだ方法である。さらに、内なるコートヤードはスラム街の路地の迷路状ネットワーク空間の延長である……が、迷路状のネットワークは平面から断面へと変換されている。

The Head of the Snake
Secret lovers arrive at the building by car, indiscreetly passing through a narrow tunnel entrance that leads to the hotel parking deep inside the block. This entrypiece is frequently a hybrid of the traditional Bangkok shophouse. However, instead of a program of retail on the street level, the bottom portion of the shophouse is hollowed out to form a street passage. The upper levels are converted into additional motel rooms linked to other units inside the blcck.

蛇の頭
秘密の恋人たちは車でやって来て、ブロックの奥深くにあるホテルの駐車場へと通じる、無用心な狭いトンネルを入る。この入り口は昔からのバンコクのショップハウスの複合体で、通りに面する店舗のプログラムに関わらず、1階はトンネルのために刳り抜かれている。ブロックの内部では、上の階では隣のモーテルまで部屋が増築されている。

old photos of nanda family home
ナンダの家族の住宅の写真

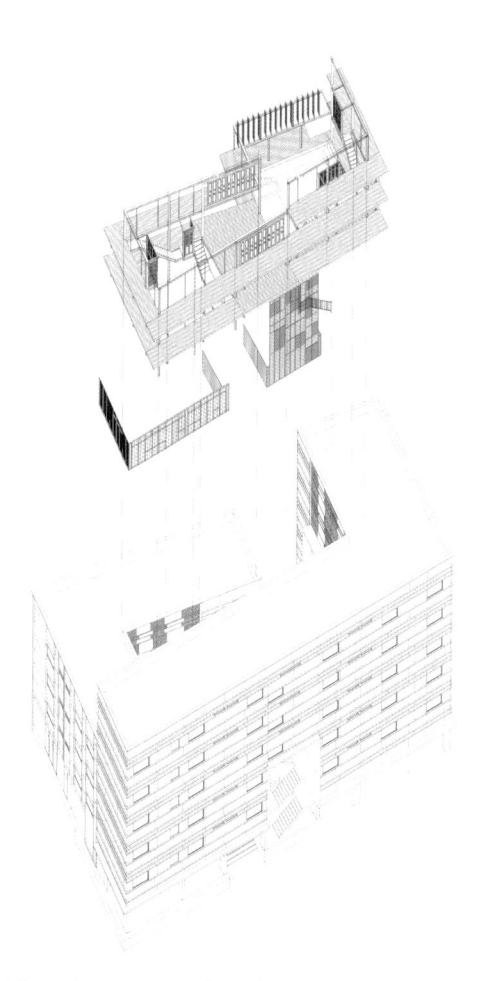

a concrete outer shell protecting an inner core of steel & wood components salvaged from nanda ancient teak familiy home....
コンクリートの外殻がスティールとナンダの家族のチーク材の家から回収された木材のインナー・コアを守っている……。

The Secret Court:
After passing through the tunnel, the vehicle surprisingly arrives in an internal court open to the sky. The car is then swiftly guided by an attendant into a private parking spot that is directly connected to a motel room.

シークレット・コート:
トンネルを抜けると突然、空に開いた中庭に出る。車はすぐに、プライベート・パーキングに誘導され、モーテルの部屋につながる。

The Curtain:
As soon as the couple has parked, a brightly colored vinyl curtain is pulled closed behind them, protecting the lovers' identity and privacy. Thus, the name *rong raam mahn rood*, or curtain motel.

カーテン：
カップルが駐車するとすぐに、原色のビニール・カーテンが閉まり、カップルのアイデンティティやプライバシーを守る。こうして、タイ語でロン・ラアム・マアン・ロオドあるいはカーテン・モーテルと呼ばれる。

view of pool court
プール・コートを見る

The Secret Passage:
The building typology of the curtain motel is completely unique in Bangkok. The majority of its archicteture is buried within an urban block, exposing only its main tunnel entry and small alley exit to the public. The building behaves like an internal street as guests can move through the entire complex inside their car.

秘密の路地空間:
バンコクでは、カーテン・モーテルの建築タイプはユニークで、建築の大部分は、都市ブロックの中に埋もれ、トンネルの入り口と、小さな路地への出口のみが露出している。客は車の中にいるままで全体を通過でき、建物は内部の路でしかないように働く。

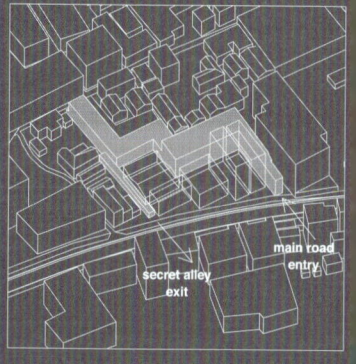

secret alley exit

main road entry

the building mass dips down to frame veiws of the neighbor's mango tree garden and shantytown beyond...
建築のマッスが下がると、マンゴーの木の庭やその向こうのスラム街がフレームの中に見える。

n section, the scale of shantytown still carries into the 7 storey courtyard with the idea of the 2-in-1 building concept.
断面では、スラム街のスケールは、ふたつがひとつになる建築コンセプトのアイディアで、7層のコートヤードに取り込まれる。

The Main Entry is a long dark tunnel through the ground floor of a shophouse, barely wide enough for one car to pass.

主入り口は、店舗の1階に通過する長く暗いトンネルで、1台の車がやっと通れる幅しかない。

tunnel entry
入り口のトンネル

The Secret Alley Exit allows for an "escape" through a side street, avoiding the jealous wife awaiting at the main entrance.

路地への秘密の出口からは、主入り口で待ちぶせている嫉妬深い妻を避け、脇の道を通って"逃亡"できる。

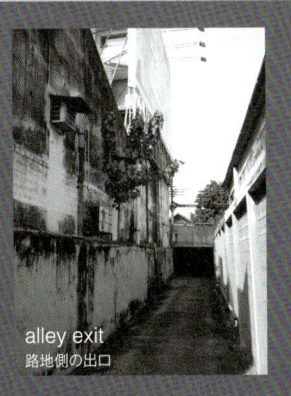

alley exit
路地側の出口

リン・ハオ

kids club / Batam Island, Indonesia / 2013
子供クラブ／インドネシア、バタム島／2013

house with mango trees / Tanah Merah, Singapore / 2014
マンゴーの木のある家／シンガポール、タナ・メラ／2014

satay by the bay (in association with kuu)
Marina Bay, Singapore / 2012
サテ・バイ・ザ・ベイ（クーとの協働）
シンガポール、マリーナベイ／2012

villa S / Sentosa Island, Singapore / 2011
ヴィラS／シンガポール、セントーサ島／2011

T house / Upper Thomson, Singapore / 2011
Tハウス／シンガポール、アッパートムソン／2011

house 11 / Geylang, Singapore / 2012
ハウス11／シンガポール、ゲイラン／2012

small worlds / Selegie, Singapore / 2007
小さな世界／シンガポール、セレギー／2007

LING Hao

Introductory Essay / Erwin VIRAY

The return to the old landscape, a perception of Singapore as new, as young, as without old tradition; yet beneath the surface there is heritage, in the tropical condition: the flow of air, of shadows and light beneath the tree foliage, creating shade and shadow, offering great relief in the hot tropics. The inside and outside re-evaluation is breathing a new life in the in-between spaces, to allow the volumes to breathe, with a manipulation of the building sections to make the humid hot atmosphere tolerable and comfortable. A new practice, alone and individual, unusual in contrast to the big teams that work in practice as the usual way things are done in a big global metropolis. Instead, Ling Hao is creating a network, a unique way of working, in the normal surroundings to attain a space for life of vital freshness. In a global place like Singapore with a flattening world seemingly the same everywhere, yet, on close inspection, there are distinct differences: in the light quality, in the gardens showing the growth of nature, letting the birds and the wind assume a role in the bringing of seeds and while water is provided by man to help in cultivating the florae in a place. The field of operation of Ling Hao is functioning like nature's flow, single and at times collaborating with others, letting things be as they should be, offering a nimble way of responding and working in this swiftly transforming world.

紹介文／エルウィン・ビライ

古き風景への回帰、新しく、若く、古い伝統のないシンガポールを感知すること。それでも表面下には、熱帯で受け継がれるものが存在する。空気の流れ、日陰をつくり熱帯では大きな慰めとなる木の葉の下の光と影。内部と外部の関係を見直すことが、内と外の中間の領域での新しい生活を蘇らせる。中間領域は、高温多湿を和らげ心地よいものにする断面的な操作を施すことによって、建物に呼吸をさせる。

大都市で通常行われるような、大きなチームで行うのとは対照的な、孤立した、個人的な新しい事務所。その代わりリン・ハオは、普通の周辺環境の中で、生き生きとした新鮮な生活のための空間を創造するために、ネットワークとユニークな仕事のやり方を編み出した。どこも皆同じように見える世界だが、シンガポールのようなグローバルな場所も、よく調べてみると、明確な違いがある。光の質、自然が成長する庭、植物を育てるために人は水やりをし、鳥や風が種子を運ぶ役割を担う。リン・ハオが操作する分野は、自然の流れのように機能し、ひとりで、そして時には協働で、物事をあるべき姿のままにし、この素早く変転する世界に適応しながら、働くための機敏な方法を提供する。

suburban landscape

In a suburban landscape built over 50 years, we can find a mix of public apartment housing, terrace houses, condominiums apartments, schools, hostels, soccer and sport fields, water reservoir, train station, hawker centre, factories. All kinds of scales and use that are linked by parks, covered walkways, open paths, roads, on a terrain that is sometimes gentle and othertimes steep. In the long past, the area was known for its red cliffs facing the sea and named Tanah Merah Kechil, but that kind of geographical aspect has been covered up by all this inhabitations. Nevertheless, there is an interesting sense of different worlds and layers that have accumulated. Walking along this or that route, there are many encounters to be found, such as an incense burning in a makeshift altar under a big tree, a cat lounging at a quiet but sunny spot, fragrances flowering plants creeping along a fence with bees buzzing around them next to a path, the feeling of relief to find a walkwa sheltering you from a sudden and heavy downpour. There is a richness of life here that is related to the outdoor and surpris and change that occurs. Coming into the homes, schools, and other such spaces, the physical relation to the exterior is mediated by roofs, walls and openings, mechanical ventilation, electronic systems and patterns of the everyday. There are continuous changes in this relationship between the indoor and outdoor with the increasingly hectic life and the apparent need control this unpredictability, to counter as it were the famous langour associated with the tropics.

郊外の風景

30年以上にわたって形成されてきた、この郊外の風景には、公共の集合住宅、テラスハウス、分譲集合住宅、学校、ホステル、サッカー競技場や運動競技場、給水タンク、鉄道駅、ホーカーセンター*、工場が混在しているのが見える。あらゆるスケール、あらゆる用途にわたる建物群である。それらは、時に緩く、時に急勾配の地形上の、公園や、覆いのある歩道、覆いのないフットパス、そして道路によって、結ばれている。

かつて長い間、この地域は海に面した赤い崖によってよく知られ、タナ・メラと呼ばれてきたが、こうした地理的な特徴は、これらの建物群によって、すっかり覆い隠されている。それでもなお、ここには幾層にも蓄積されてきた、何だか面白そうな、他とは違う感じの世界が存在している。

ここここのルートを歩いてみると、さまざまな出来事に出合う。大きな樹の下に置かれた仮の祭壇で焚かれるお香の香り、静寂な陽溜まりの中を歩きまわる猫、道路のフェンス沿いに漂ってくる芳しい花の香り、その花の周りには、ブンブン飛び回る蜜蜂、突然の土砂降りの雨に、覆いのあるウォークウェイを見つけて、ほっとする感覚。ここにはある種の生活の豊かさがある。それは外部空間に関係し、そこで起きる予測しないことや、思いがけないこと、変わったことに関係している。家々や、学校や、その他の空間の内部では、屋根や外壁、開口部、換気設備、電子的なシステム、毎日の生活のパターンがあることによって、外部に対する身体的な関係は緩和される。

外部空間と内部空間のこうした関係は、絶え間なく、変化し続けている。ますます増大する生活の消費と、予測できないことを、コントロールしなければならないという必要と、いわゆる熱帯特有の倦怠を、抑えこまなければならないという必要と共に。

*ホーカーセンター：廉価な飲食店の屋台や店舗を集めた屋外複合施設

Section. Floors are arranged as open terraces overlapping the other stepping up through the house. 1:150

house with mango trees / 2014

This is a house in such a suburban landscape.
A mature mango tree is to be be found at both ends of this oblong terrac plot measuring 6 x 35m. Open spaces step up alternately through the house over 4 floors while being next to these big trees; dining in the garden below the tree, watching tv and chatting in the living room next to the leaves and fruits and looking out at the crown of the tree from the corridor. Inside the house, the floors are like stepping terraces which gen tly curve away and overlook the other, at the same time bringing daylight in and flow of fresh breezes through. With facings towards the east and west, sunlight moves through the openings between the floor terraces and party walls from the morning to the evening.

With this gaps or openings, the different spaces have multi directional aspects and relations. Movable wall panels allow the spaces to flow freel Adjoining these are small gardens, some open to the rain, leading to a gently rising roof garden. From here, the openness of the roof garden planted with various kinds of grasses under the big sky relate to the scale of the apartment blocks, schools and soccer field surrounding this imme-diate enclave of terrace houses, in the midst of a steep valley. The experi ence here is to come across sounds or silence of the house and the stree sunlight or shade of the cloud, views of the mango trees and surrounding daily activities or gusts of winds. The feeling is of openess and being part of the outside environment even when you are deep inside the house.

断面　フロアはオープンテラスとして重なりながらスキップして、だんだん上っていく。1:150

マンゴーの木のある家／2014

これは、そうした郊外の風景の中にある、住宅である。
この6m×35mの敷地に建つ細長い長方形のテラスハウスの両端には、大きく成長したマンゴーの樹が植わっている。この大きな樹に接して、家全体の4層にわたって、さまざまなオープンスペースが、互い違いに上っていく。──樹の下の庭にあるダイニング、マンゴーの葉や果実のすぐ横のリビングでは、テレビを見たり、お喋りをしたり、そして廊下からは、樹のてっぺん越しに外が見渡せる。家の中は、フロアは曲線を描き、段々のテラスのようにスキップして、他のフロアを下に見る。同時に互い違いのフロアの間からは光が射し込み、新鮮な空気が流れ込む。東と西に面しているために、スキップするフロアの隙間、間仕切り壁の隙間から、朝から晩まで日光が射し込む。

この隙間や開口によって、それぞれの異なる空間には多面的な方向性や関係性が生まれる。可動の間仕切りによって、自由な空間の流れが生まれる。それらに接してさまざまな小さな庭があり（庭によっては雨が降り込む庭もある）、緩やかに盛り上がったルーフ・ガーデンへと通じる。
いろいろな種類の草が植えられ、大空の下にルーフ・ガーデンが開いていることによって、急峻な谷間にぽつんと投げ込まれたこのテラスハウスは、中心にあるアパートメント・ブロックや学校、サッカー場の規模と関連付けられる。ここでは家と道路の騒音と静寂、日の光と雲の影、そしてマンゴーの木とその周りの景色、毎日の生活と一陣の突風が交差するといった経験が生まれる。家の奥深くに沈潜している時でさえも周囲の環境の一部であるという感覚、開いている感覚を感じられる。

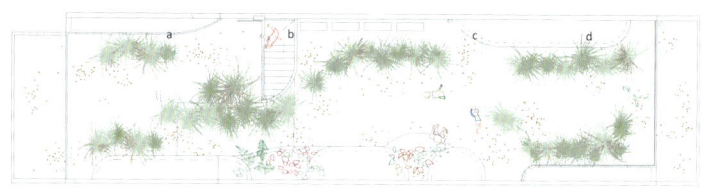

Roof garden. A variety of grasses are planted on a thin layer of crushed rock. Over time, the wind and birds bring many other plants to slowly make kind of a natural garden.

ルーフ・ガーデン。砕石の薄い層にさまざまな種類の草が植えられている。時間が経って、風と鳥が他の植物の種子を多く運んでくるので、だんだんと野生の庭のようになりつつある。

3rd storey plan. Permeable steel mesh corridors allow many paths around the different spaces.

3階平面図。透過性のスティール・メッシュの通路を通って、異なる空間へと通じる。

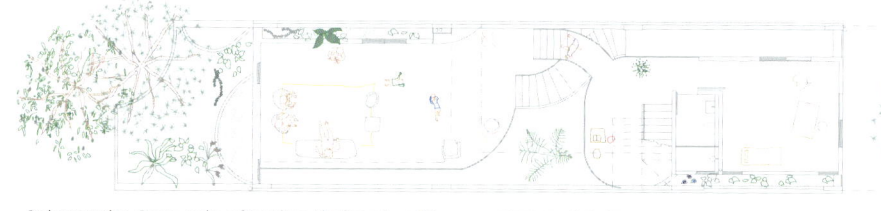

2nd storey plan. Curves make softer edges. The floors have thin gardens on one side open to the rain and gaps on the other.

2階平面図。曲線が柔らかいエッジをつくる。フロアの一方の端には、雨の当たる幅の狭い庭があり、もう一方の端の床にはスリットがある。

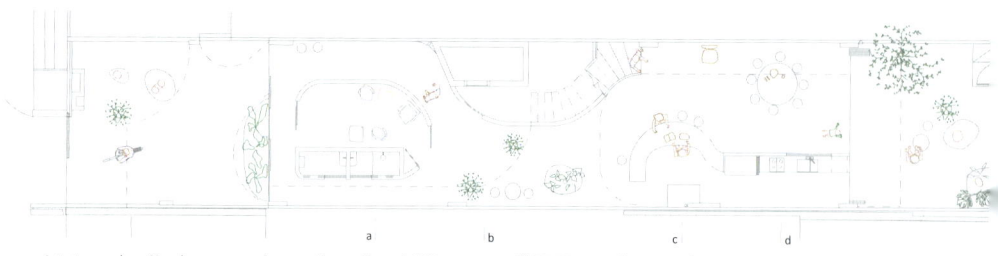

1st storey plan. Simple curves make a continous flow. 1:270

1階平面図。シンプルなカーブから連続する流れが生まれる。1:270

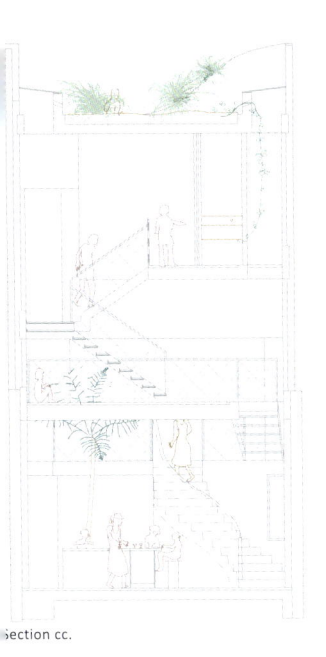

Section cc. 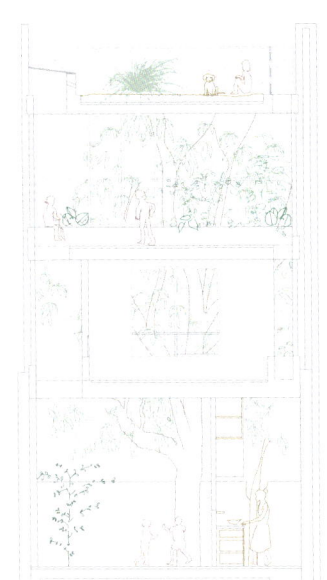   Section dd.

Section aa.    Section bb.

Air, light and sounds circulate freely around the house through gaps or steel mesh floors of 500mm to 1000mm between the floors and boundary walls of the house.
Going from the lower level to the roof garden, it is like taking a walk along a hilly landscape with new aspects at each turn. Moving here or there, the relation to the natural light, wind, views or openess changes. While indoors, each day will feel different with the natural conditons ever changing. We can imagine the spaces being open to and accomodating different situations or uses.

床と界壁の間に、500mmから1000mmの床のギャップやスティール・メッシュの床があることで、家中に空気、光、音の自由な流れが生まれる。
下層階からルーフ・ガーデンまで上っていくと、まるで丘の地形を歩いているような、そこここに違った表情を発見する。あちらこちらに移動すると、自然の光や風との関係、眺望や外への開き方の割合が変化していく。内部であるのに、外部の自然の状態の変化に伴って、毎日が異なって感じられる。異なる状況や使い方をされたとしても、これらの空間は対応できると思える。

shophouses
house 11 / 2012

This is an area with shophouses dating back to the 1920s. Built to accomodate commercial activities on the lower level and housing on the upper, they would be gridded into blocks by busy streets and quieter backlanes. They are typically 2 level with a covered footway fronting the main street and have a L shape plan around a rear outdoor courtyard. At the moment, these buildings house homes, shops, eateries, offices, clan houses, brothels and others. While outwardly the buildings are conserved and remain the same, the interiors and the streets are continously been used in different ways.

ショップハウス
ハウス11／2012

ここは1920年代までさかのぼれる店舗付き住宅のある地域である。店舗付き住宅は、賑やかな表通りと静かな裏路に挟まれたグリッド状の敷地に建てられ、下階に商業施設、上階に住宅のある建物である。メイン・ストリートに面して覆い付きの歩廊がついた通常2層の建物で、背後の中庭を囲み、L型をしている。今のところ、これらの建物には住居、店舗、料理店、宿屋、風俗店、などが入っている。外観は保存され、同じ表情をしているが、内部と街路は常にさまざまな異なる使われ方をしてきた。

1:850

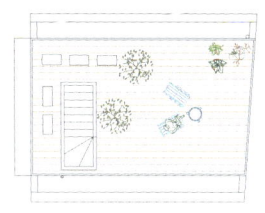

roof terrace plan

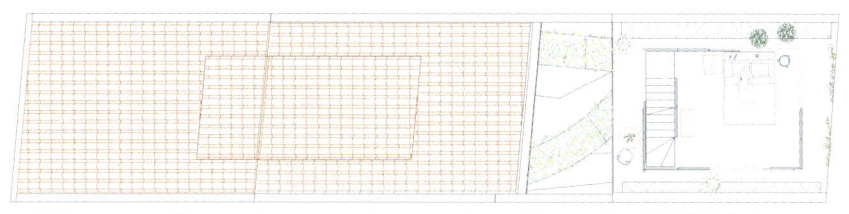

roof /4th storey plan. Sliding open the glass doors, the rear becomes an open terrace amongst the rooftops and surroundings.

ルーフと4階平面図。ガラスの引戸を開け放つと、増築部分は周辺より高いオープンテラスになる。

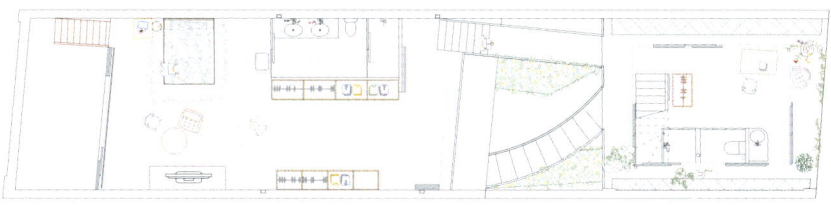

mezzanine /3rd storey plan. A timber mezzanine is inserted within the envelope of the old pitch roof to the front. A new stair connecting to the mezzanine in the front allows a continous path through the whole shophouse.

中3階／3階平面図。道路側の既存の勾配屋根の建物の中に、木造の中3階が挿入された。前面の中3階に上る新たな階段によって、「ショップハウス」全体に人の流れができた。

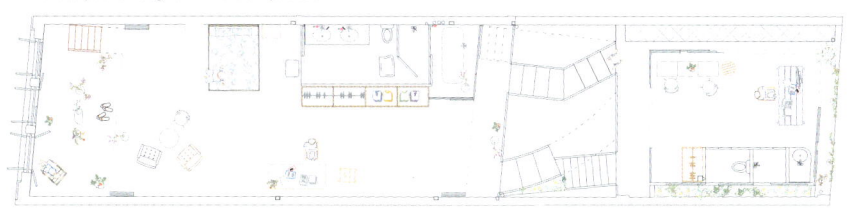

2nd storey plan. A route is made around an open courtyard connecting the extension, built at half levels, with the existing portion along a meandering steel stairs sheltered by hanging plants.

2階平面図。開いた中庭の回りに、レベルを半層ずつずらして、増築部分と既存部分を曲がりくねったスティールの階段で結ぶルートがつくられた。階段は観葉植物のハンギングバスケットで覆われている。

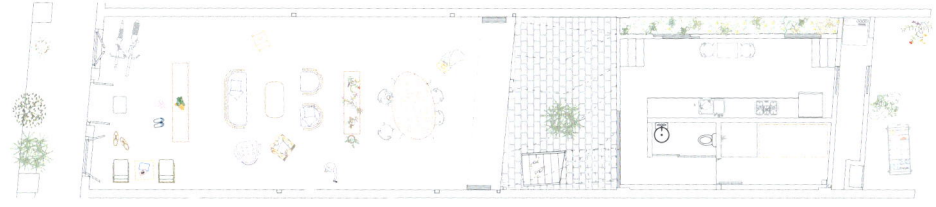

1st storey plan. 1:230
This is a project about enlarging the spaces as well making it more open to itself and to the surroundings. To the rear of this shophouse, a compact 4 level tower is inserted; 7m long x 4m wide x 13m high surrounded by diffused light and air, in contrast to the enclosed existing front portion.

平面図 1:230
空間を拡げる、内側に対しても周辺の外側にも、空間をよりオープンなものにしようとするプロジェクトである。この店舗付き住宅の背後に、コンパクトな4層のタワーが挿入された。長さ7m×幅4m×高さ13mのタワーで、閉鎖的な既存部とは対照的に、拡散する光と空気に囲まれている。

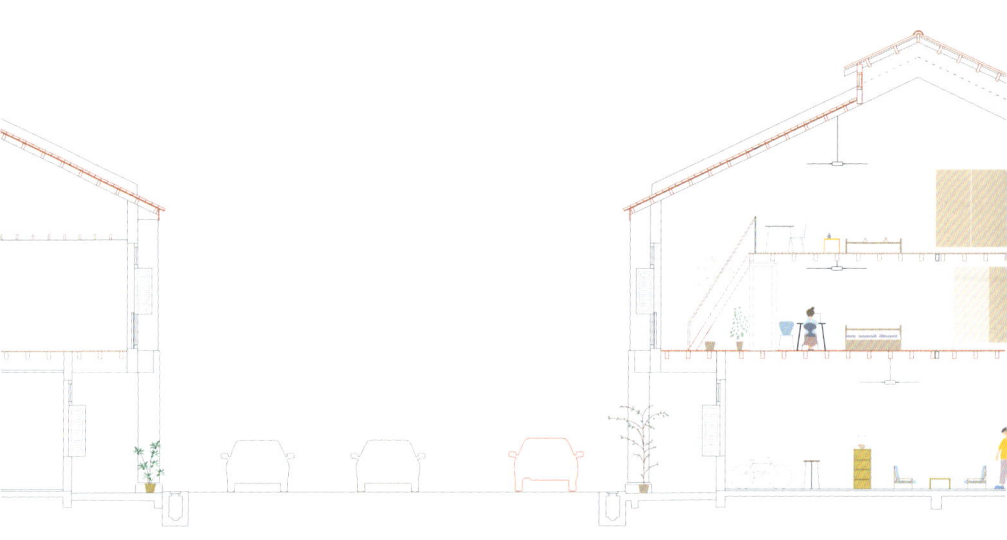

section across street and house 11 and apartment block across backlane. 1:210
通りとハウス11、アパートメントブロックと裏通りの横断面図。1:210

climbing a hanging garden ハンギングガーデンを上ると

Short stairs connect the staggered levels in many ways. Over these stairs, shelters also become planters for hanging gardens. The effect is of walking around a suspended garden which rustles gently when the breeze flows through or the pitter patter of the rain drops.

ジグザグにずらした床レベルを、短い階段たちがさまざまな形態で繋いでいる。これらの階段の上では、覆い屋根も、ハンギングガーデンのためのプランターになっている。そのため、このハンギングガーデンを歩き回るとき、吹き抜ける風に葉叢はサラサラと鳴り、雨が降れば雨音はパタパタと響く。

63

Plan drawing of a neighbourhood of compact terrace houses built in mid 20th century. The land plots are usually 6m x 28m. They were all built as one storey houses on a valley next to a nature reserve and water catchment area from the 19th century. New families or developers have bought over individual plots and are transforming them to 3 or 4 level houses. The T House owner has a different ambition, he wants to make a small house where he can grow plants.

20世紀半ばに建てられたコンパクトなテラスハウス群地区の平面図。敷地の区画は通常6m×28mである。19世紀以来の自然保護区と集水池のある地域に隣接する谷に、すべて、平屋のテラスハウスとして建てられた。ニューファミリーやディベロッパーが個々の敷地を買い占め、これらを3階から4階の住宅に改装している。このTハウスのオーナーには少し違った望みがあって、植物を育てられる家をつくりたいと望んだ。

house with plants
T house / 2011

The house is a few small rooms arranged around gardens and plants. Simple brick walls and slender steel and concrete structures form the intimate spaces with big openings and carry a roof garden. There is a closeness between the everyday and the natural with the proximity of things to one another, from the furnitures to the plants and surroundings.

植物と共にある住宅
Tハウス／2011

庭と植物の回りに配された、いくつかの小さな部屋からなる住宅である。シンプルな煉瓦の壁と細身のスティールと鉄筋コンクリートの構造で、大きな開口とルーフガーデンをもつ居心地の良いスペースをつくり出している。椅子やテーブルと周囲の植物が近くにあり、日常と自然が隣り合っている。

1:260

66   Section. 1:200. House is rebuilt following the profile of the land.   断面　家は土地の断面に沿って建つ。 1:200

closeness

Small rooms overlook this courtyard space of 5m long x 6m wide x 5.7m high. It is indoors yet airy and open to the surroundings. Here, the sounds of the tv mingle with the chirping of the birds, the chatter of the neigbours while you cook and eat or surf the internet. Here, also the owner is constantly at work on his gardens.

親密さ

いくつかの小さな部屋が縦5m×幅6m×高さ5.7mの中庭を見下ろす。ここは内部空間なのだが、風通しが良く周囲に対して開いている。料理をしている時、食事をしている時、ネットサーフィンをしている時、テレビの音に鳥のさえずり、隣人たちのお喋りが、交じり合い、聞こえてくる。オーナーは仕事を、いつもここで、彼の庭でしている。

satay by the bay / 2012
(in association with kuu)

Drawing of the hawker centre on a saturday night. Around the clusters of cooking stalls, visitors and furniture congregate casually, inside and outside and amongst the plants.

A project for a food hawker centre on the southern waterfront of Singapore, it is also next to a freshly built public gardens. Various waterbodies surround the site holding and filtering the rain water before it goes to the reservoir. Making this place involves planting trees, extending ponds and building numerous pathways.

・テ・バイ・ザ・ベイ／2012
ーとの協働)

曜の夜のホーカーセンターのド
ーイング。そこここにある調理エ
アの周辺では、植物に挟まれて、
外に、利用客とテーブル、椅子
思い思いに集まっている。

ンガポール南部のウォーターフ
ントにある、フード・ホーカーセ
ターのプロジェクト。ここも最近
設された公共の庭園に隣接して
る。敷地の周りにある池や川が、
水地に行く前の雨水を集め、ま
浄化する。この場所をつくる仕
には、植物を植え、池を広げ、無
の歩行路をつくることが含まれ
いる。

tropical hat

A concrete roof curves in and out and dips down at various ends in relation to plants and outdoor seating areas to make a shaded and open canopy. Food and drink stalls are arranged in clusters allowing a simple and continous movement and surrounded by eating areas that are next to the plants or water. Many paths lead into and from the hawker centre making an experience where the visitor moves through plants, food stalls, seatings, smells, gatherings and conversations and an atmosphere that contrasts from smoky to breezy, boisterous to the calm.The concrete canopy is 4.5m high and dips down to 2.2m and this extends with hanging plants including wedelia, russelia and vernonia elliptica making a natural curtain of different densities draping onto the ground. Immediately around, the canopies continue with 30 to 40m high dense verdant angsana trees, 10m h singular palm trees, 30m high wrangly flowering trumpet trees, spreading tiered pagoda shaped 25m h sea almond trees and many other kinds of plants.

熱帯の帽子

内に外にカーブしたコンクリートの屋根が、植物と屋外の客席エリアとの関係を保ちながら、端部は下方に傾斜し、日陰をつくり、オープン・キャノピーをつくり出す。フードとドリンクの売場を集めて配置することによって、シンプルで流れるような動線が生まれ、飲食エリアに囲まれ、飲食エリアは植物と池や川に隣接する。ホーカーセンターの中のたくさんの通路が、ひとつの体験をつくり出す。つまり利用客は、植物や、屋台やテーブル、椅子、匂い、人びと、会話の間を通り抜ける。それは、静寂とは対照的な、煙で霞む、快活で、騒然とした雰囲気である。コンクリートのキャノピーは高さが4.5mから2.2mまで垂れ下がり、その上にはウェデリア、ラッセリア、ヴァーノイア・エリプティカなどのハンギング植物が植えられ、それがさまざまな密度の自然のカーテンになり、地面に垂れ下がっている。すぐ隣接するキャノピーに続いて鬱蒼とし、青々とした30mから40mのアングサナ・ツリーや10mの1本の広がった椰子の木、3mmの花盛りのトランペット・ツリー、段状に重なるパゴダの形をした25mの高さのシー・アーモンド・ツリー、その他のたくさんの種類の植物が途切れることなく植えられている。

Section. 1:180 A shady, cool, porous space made from canopies of trees and concrete roofs.
木々のキャノピーとコンクリートの屋根が木陰をつくる、涼しく、風通しのよい空間。

From the interior, to the open spaces and to the exterior under the big shades, the feeling is cool and fresh. This would be a suitable way to make spaces in the tropics, shaded structures extending to and from big trees continously, plants and other natural surroundings and buildings mixing to create a comfortable atmosphere.

インテリアからオープンスペースまで、そして大きな日陰の中のエクステリアまで、感じられるのは涼しさと新鮮さである。日陰をつくる構造体を大きな木々に連続してつくり、植物や自然環境と建物をミックスし、快適な環境をつくり出すことは、熱帯で空間をつくり出す上での適切な方法であると思う。

Site 1:2250

kids club / 2013

As part of a beach resort in Batam Island facing the Singapore Straits, a slender building 5m wide x 35m long is made curving around a circular pool. A place for kids of all ages to play, there are small intimate bunks to open platforms arranged in relation to a continous path from a zig zagging ramp to a bamboo climb. The building is made from a 150mm diam bamboo structure, finished with bamboo in various ways and reacts continously to the user or the environment. The effect is like playing in a soft and natural atmosphere that you become part of.

子供クラブ／2013

バタム島のシンガポール海峡に面するビーチ・リゾートの一部として、円形のプールに沿ってカーブした、幅5m×長さ35mの細長い建物がつくられた。あらゆる年齢の子供たちが遊べる場所で、ジグザグ蛇行する斜路からバンブーの階段に続く通路に沿って配置された開放的なプラットフォームに小さな居心地の良い寝床がある。この建物は直径150mmの竹の構造で出来ていて、仕上げにもバンブーがさまざまな形で使われている。バンブーは使う人や環境に対して持続的に順応する。柔らかく、自然の雰囲気の中で、その一部になって遊んでいるような効果がある。

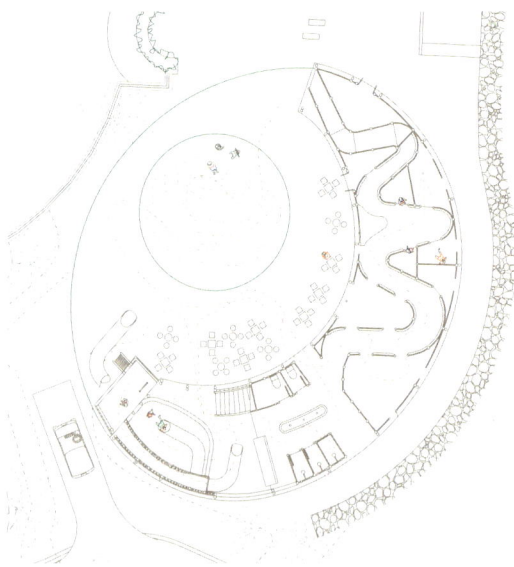

1st storey plan. 1:400
The bamboo columns are arranged at 2.5m spacing to carry the level above while making enclosures for the play areas. The roof structure is a simple portal frame with twin splaying columns at both ends.

バンブーの柱は2.5m間隔で設置され、上の階を支え、プレイエリアの囲いにもなっている。屋根は両端の斜めの双子柱で支えられたシンプルな門型フレームの構造である。

2nd storey plan. 1:350
A open cool thin space generously shaded by the thatch roof.

開放的で涼しい、細長い空間で、茅葺屋根が十分な日陰をつくり出す

pliant

The floor moves gently in response when walked on. The building assembled from different parts of bamboo is flexible yet strong. Strips are stretched in various curves to hold together bamboo poles or tie together the poles to form the frame. The monsoon squalls which comes at the end of the year flows through the building. Equally pliant are the deft hands of the builders who come from Bali bringing with them the bamboo and rapidly assemble the portal frame, weave the different spaces, and lay the thatched roof.

しなやか

床はその上を歩くに従って、緩やかに揺れる。バンブーの異なった部位から出来ているこの建物は柔軟であり、強くもある。細い部材をさまざまなカーブに伸ばし、一緒にして竹柱を支え、柱を結束して、フレームをつくる。1年の終わりに来るモンスーンのスコールは建物を突き抜けて流れる。同じようにしなやかなのは手先の器用なバリから来た職人たちで、バンブーも一緒に運んで来て、素早く門型フレームを組み立て、茅葺屋根を葺きあげる。

1st storey plan. 1:675. The house does not appear to have a front or back but curves continuously as you walk around it from the roads surrounding it to the waterway. Inside amidst the openess the floors slope gently towards the middle area.

1階平面図1:675　この家には前面と背面というものがなく、周りを歩いて、水路に囲まれた道路から見るとカーブだけが連続して見える。開放的な内部では、床は中の方に向かって緩やかに傾斜している。

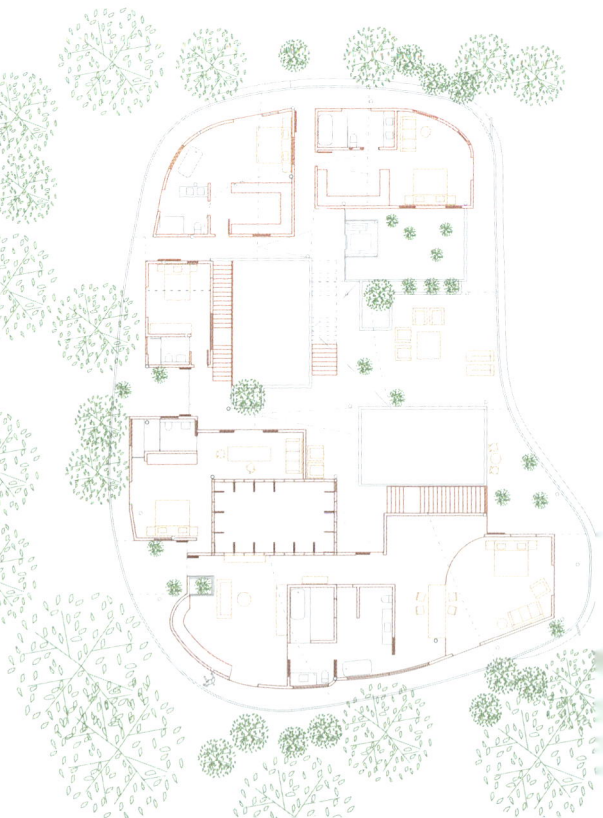

2nd storey plan. 1:425. The floor slopes gently towards the view of the waterways. A verandah following the curving perimeter bring the exterior into the spaces of timber enclosures and continues to the pathways linking them. The sea breeze permeates through this open interior.

2階平面図 1:425　床面は水路が見える方に向かって緩く傾斜している。周辺部に合わせてカーブしたベランダは囲われた木の空間に外部をもち込み、その内部を結ぶ通路へと繋がって行く。海からの風はこの開放的なインテリアを通り抜ける。

villa S / 2011

The site is on a man made extension to a small island where many villas have been built as part of a community where they share open land and waterways. The villa is where a few families would come to gather away from the city. The scale of the house is like that of an environment, containing the experience of the surroundings. 4 large courtyards are placed inside connecting all the levels to the sky and rain. The enclosures and openings have an equal sense of proportions in this house.

ヴィラS／2011

敷地は、小さな島の埋立地にある。そこでは空地や水路を共有するひとつのコミュニティを形成する多くのヴィラが建設されてきた。このヴィラは数組の家族が都会から離れて、リラックスし、交遊するためにやって来る所である。家の規模は、周辺のヴィラとだいたい同じだが、周辺の体験の部分も含んでいる。内部に配された大きな4つの中庭は、各階を結び付け、空へと開き、雨が降り込む。囲まれた部分と開かれた部分が、同じ割合でこの家は構成されている。

Roof terrace plan and view. 1:300
Under an expansive sky, a continous undulating landscape of a grassy knoll, floating meshes of hanging plants, timber platforms and a swimming pool along the edge facing towards the sea.

ルーフ・テラスの平面図と眺望 1:300
広々とした空の下で、草の小山や、ハンギング植物の浮遊するメッシュや、木製の床面からなる起伏のあるランドスケープ、そして海の方向に面した、建物のエッジにあるスイミング・プール。

The floors are sloping; making highs and lows, gently rolling strolls, steel climbs or sliight depressions. These relate to the different surroundings, being under the sky, sloping with the view toward the cove on the 2nd storey or sloping inwards on the 1st storey. With the different slopes overlapping the other the spaces open up in many directions.

Moving around this house is to walk amidst many unfolding sceneries.

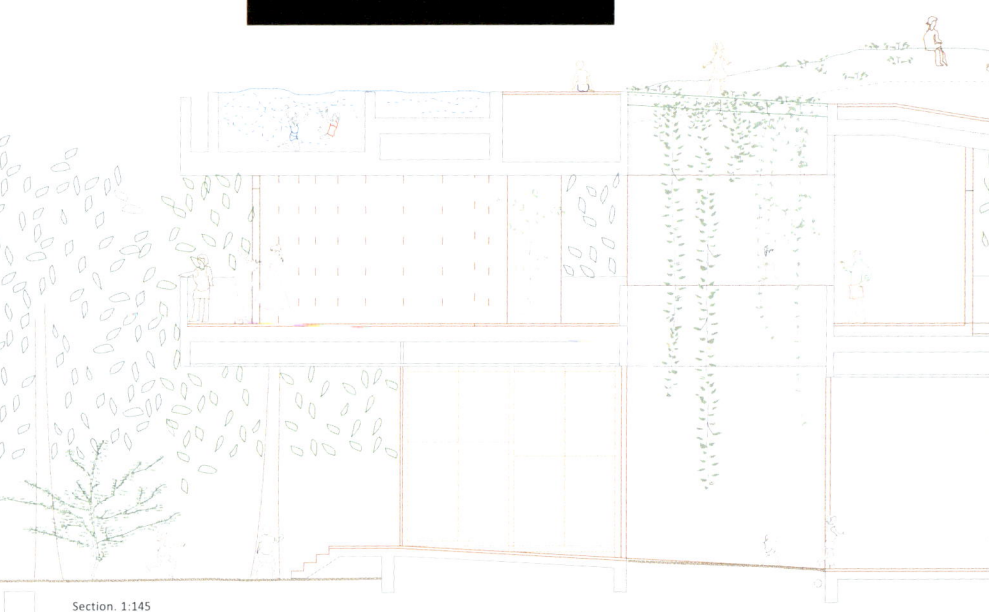

Section. 1:145

床面は傾斜している。高い所や低い所をつくり出し、歩面は緩やかにうねり、スティール階段を、あるいはちょっとした凹みをつくる。これらは異なった周辺と関わりがある。空の下で、2階では入江の眺望に向かって傾斜し、1階では内向きに傾斜する。異なるスロープが他のスロープと重なり合い、空間が、さまざまな方向に開いていく。この家の中を動き回ることは、いろいろなシーンが展開する中を歩くことである。

roof terrace

4th storey plan

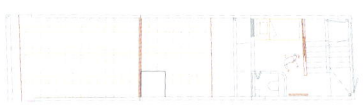

3rd storey plan

2nd storey plan

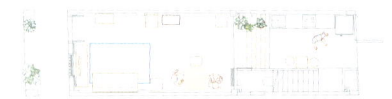

1st storey plan. 1:300

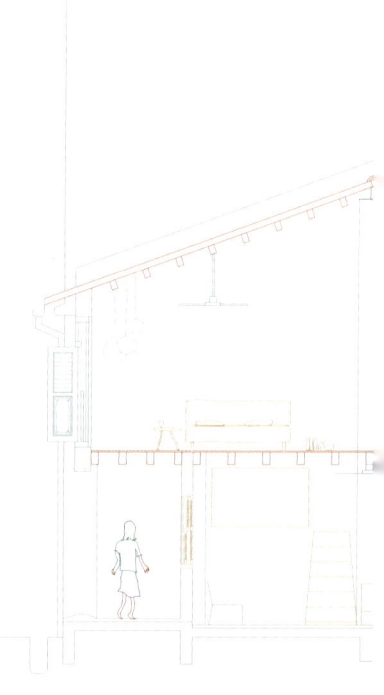

Section. 1:125

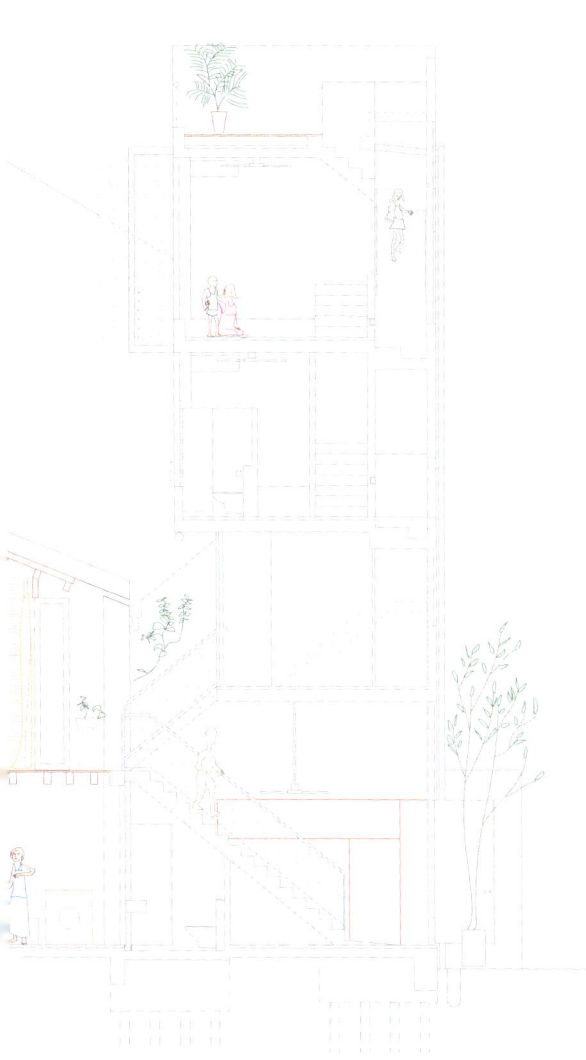

small worlds
2007

The site measures 3.6 m x 15m.
To a 2 storey terrace shophouse that was built in the 1920s, a rear extension of 4 storeys with a roof terrace is added. The house is transformed to a series of small rooms, one after the other horizontally and then vertically. A smaller and more intimate sense of dimension and scale is made, where the limits of the space are always felt in relation to the everyday life.

小さな世界
2007

敷地は3.6m×15m。1920年代に建てられた２階建ての店舗付きのテラスハウスの背後に足された、ルーフ・テラスのある４階建ての増築棟。この家は、一連の小さな部屋をひとつずつ水平方向に並べ、そのあと垂直方向に転換したものである。毎日、生活する中で、空間の境界がいつも感じられるような、より小さな、より居心地の良い寸法とスケールの感覚でつくられた。

inside

The stair, bathroom, laundry and storage are arranged around a small space of 3.6m x 4m. It is also next to the outside , the sky and exposed to the changes of the weather conditions. When you wash your face in the morning light, it will also be with the sounds of the streets. The small house is even more a part of the city.

In the tropics, things left on their own will naturally transform and be overgrown with plants. That is how everyday relations could be like, a world where mixing and casualness is pervasive.

A way of making with the physical environment would be about how much to leave open, how much to connect or how much to just let be.

内部

3.6m×4mの小さな空間に階段、浴室、洗濯室、収納が配置されている。この空間は外部そして空と近接し、天候の変化に曝されている。朝の光の中で顔を洗う時、街路の音も聞こえてくる。小さな家は都市の一部以上でさえある。

熱帯では、物事は自分の意志に任され、自然に変貌し、植物と共に伸びすぎてしまう。毎日の関係はこんな風に、混合と偶然がねじ曲がった世界である。

ここでの物理的な環境をつくるひとつの方法は、どれだけオープンなままにできるか、どれだけ結び付けることができるか、あるいはまた、どれだけあるがままにしておくことができるか、に掛かっているのだと思う。

Acknowledgement

Our deep gratitude to those who collaborated and contributed to the projects as well as this exhibition.

Kuu - Satoko Saeki
      Tan Kok Meng

Ang Wei Xiong
Sheila Caterina
Chan Hui Min
Keith Chen
Ee Hui Jie
Fong Kian Kwok
Huang XuLi
Joel Lau
Adeline Koh
Lim Zhi Rui
Lin Huiying
Sky Lo
Low Ming Fang
Ngu Ping Wei
Ong Hui Loh
Denise Tan
Tay Yew
Tey Khang Siang
Samantha Wong
Yap Shan Ming
Xin Miao
Zi Yan

ヴォ・チョン・ギア

Son La Restaurant / Son La, Vietnam / 2014
ソンラ・レストラン／ベトナム、ソンラ／2014

Bamboo Wing / Vinh Phuc, Vietnam / 2009
バンブー・ウィング／ベトナム、ヴィンフック／2009

Wind and Water Bar / Binh Duong, Vietnam / 2008
ウィンド・アンド・ウォーター・バー／ベトナム、ビンズン／2008

Stacking Green(2011), House for Trees(2014) / Ho Chi Minh City, Vietnam
スタッキング・グリーン（2011）、ハウス・フォー・ツリー（2014）
ベトナム、ホーチミンシティ

Farming Kindergarten / Dong Nai, Vietnam / 2013
ファーミング・キンダーガーテン／ベトナム、ドンナイ／2013

Milan Expo Pavilion / Milan, Italy / 2015
ミラノ万博パヴィリオン／イタリア、ミラノ／2015

VO Trong Nghia

Introductory Essay / Erwin VIRAY

"Air, water, nature" are the first words encountered upon entering the VO Trong Nghia Architecture studio in Ho Chin Minh City. The space is pristine, quiet, immaculate, and serene. It seems meditation is practiced to be in state of mind to imagine clearly a quality of life. This calm serenity is a contrast to the chaos and noise of the outside world of the city.

Years ago, my attention was first captured by how VO Trong Nghia used bamboo, how the choice of a material to make architecture offer a challenge to understanding what it is to build in Vietnam, to reflect a condition of a place. It is a bold proposition on what architecture can do to create an environment, through a method of construction, through the material and detail, to make an economically responsive and sustainable structure and space. In a hot humid climate the exploration of natural ventilation in space is an opportunity to show us how air, water and nature can help create environments to re-imagine the possible in the resources we have and create a sustainable and transcendent place in a fast moving chaotic world.

紹介文／エルウィン・ビライ

"空気、水、自然"が、ホーチミンシティのヴォ・チョン・ギアの建築スタジオに入った時に最初に出合った言葉である。その空間は素朴で、静かで、清潔で、穏やかであった。人生の特質を明確に思い描く心の状態になるための、メディテーションが実践されているように見える。この静かな平穏さは、この都市の外の世界における混沌と騒音とは対照的である。

数年前、最初に私が注目したのは、ヴォ・チョン・ギアのバンブーの扱い方であり、ベトナムにおいて敷地の状況を考慮し、どんな建物が建てられるべきかを考えながら、材料を選定していることである。経済性を考慮し、持続可能な構造、空間をつくるために、工法、材料とディテールを通して、環境をつくり出すために建築に何が可能かということへの、ひとつの大胆な提案である。高温多湿の気候の中で、自然換気を考えることによって、空気、水、自然が、われわれのもっている資源の可能性をもう一度考えさせ、どんな風に環境をつくり出すかを示すひとつの機会を与えている。そして、素早く移りゆく混沌とした世界の中に、持続可能な、卓越した場所をつくり出している。

Save Our Earth

There are more than 7 billion people living on our planet, and this number increases every day. Population growth causes massive problems for tropical Asian countries, and Vietnam is no exception. The population of Vietnam now exceeds 90 million, and it is said that it will surpass 100 million by the year 2020. In Ho Chi Minh City, the largest city in Vietnam, the 7.8 million citizens collectively own a staggering 4.2 million motorbikes. This overabundance of motorbikes is causing chronic traffic congestion and serious air pollution. Similar situations where urban development is actually harmful to the everyday lives of citizens are happening all across the country. The impact that tropical Asian countries inflict on the global environment is rapidly intensifying, however, these countries have great potential in saving our Earth if only the people would change their mindsets. As architects working amid a tropical concrete jungle, we are constantly considering what we can do to benefit our planet. Although it may not be possible to stop the global population explosion, we can employ more sustainable building methods and, with a little imagination, we can develop urban areas without depriving them of greenery. We use bamboo for construction because we regard it as more environmentally sustainable than anything else. We adopt greenery into our designs because we think doing so is an opportunity to heal our battered Earth.

私たちの地球には70億を超える人びとが住んでおり、その数は日々増加している。人口増加は熱帯アジア諸国に大規模な問題をもたらしており、ベトナムも例外ではない。ベトナムの人口はいまや9,000万人を超え、2020年には1億を超えると言われている。最大の都市ホーチミンシティでは、780万人の市民が420万台を超えるバイクを所有しているが、この途方もない数を想像できるだろうか。あふれかえるバイクは慢性的な交通渋滞や深刻な大気汚染を引き起こし、いわば都市の発展がかえって市民の生活を損なうといった状態が、国内の至るところで起こっている。

熱帯アジアが与える地球環境への負荷は、急速な増大の途上にある。しかしその分、人びとの考え方が変わりさえすれば、地球を救うポテンシャルも高いということでもある。私たちは、熱帯のコンクリートジャングルの真ん中に活動する建築家として、地球のために何ができるのかということを常に思考している。私たちは地球規模の人口爆発を食い止めることはできないかもしれないが、今後の建設をサステイナブルに実行することはできる。また、工夫次第で都市からグリーンを奪うことなく開発を進めることも可能である。私たちが建設にバンブーを使用するのは、それが他の何よりも環境に対してサステイナブルだと考えているからである。私たちがデザインにグリーンを採り入れるのは、それが疲弊した地球を回復する契機だととらえているからである。

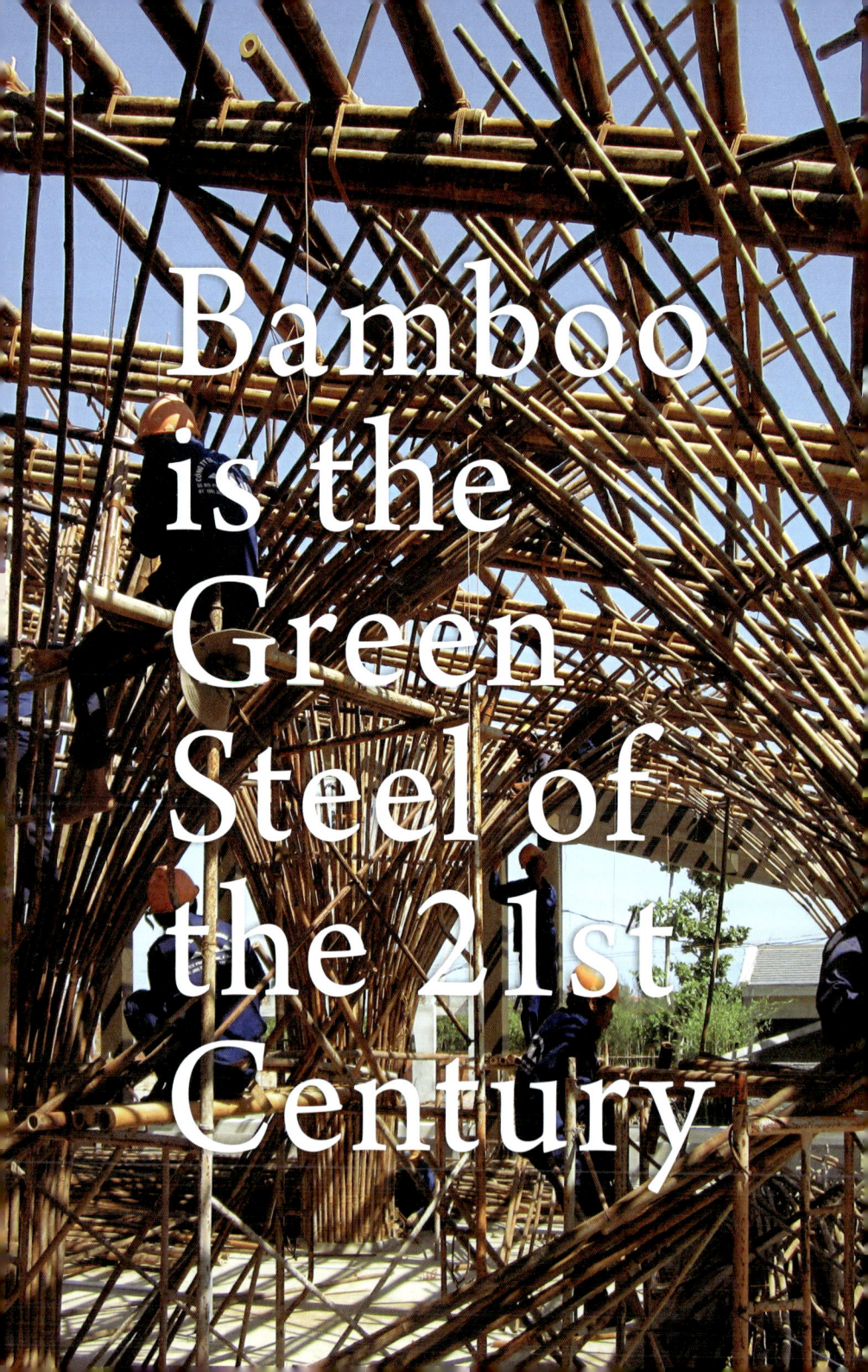

Bamboo is the Green Steel of the 21st Century

The three materials that impelled 20th century architecture are steel, concrete, and glass. These materials have extended the possibilities of architecture in developed nations, but the same cannot necessarily be said for other nations. Concrete and brick construction is still dominant in developing nations; however, these construction methods have several negative environmental consequences. For example, the cement and brick industries discharge huge amounts of carbon dioxide, and using such materials contributes to the heat island effect in cities.

We have been continuously using bamboo in the construction of numerous restaurants, schools, and resorts in Vietnam. Bamboo has the remarkable ability to grow rapidly and absorb CO_2, and it is also lightweight and has a material strength comparable to that of steel. As such, bamboo is worthy of being called the green steel of the 21st century. Trees typically used for construction need at least 10 years of growing time, whereas bamboo can be used after just 3 years. In other words, we can minimize the negative impact on forests by using bamboo instead of timber. Although we do apply several traditional construction methods in our bamboo architecture, our aim is not to reproduce the vernacular, but to create sustainable architecture suited to the present. In order for us to do this, it is essential that we systematize the production and construction of bamboo architecture.

Our Earth is already wearing thin; large-scale deforestation and rampant urbanization must be slowed down. The architecture of tomorrow must not only lessen its impact on the environment, but also rebuild the natural environment. We believe that bamboo architecture can contribute to reforestation and play a vital role in achieving this goal.

20世紀の建築をリードしたのは鉄、コンクリート、ガラスという3つの材料である。これらの材料は先進国において建築の可能性を大いに広げたかもしれないが、その他の国々では必ずしもそうとは言えない。開発途上国では鉄筋コンクリートと煉瓦による建設が現在も支配的であるが、この構法はいくつかの環境的問題をはらんでいる。例えば、セメント産業や煉瓦の製造は大量のCO_2を排出し、そのような材料で建設された都市はヒートアイランド現象にさいなまれている。

私たちはベトナムにおいて、多くのレストランや学校、リゾート施設等の建設にバンブーを使用している。バンブーは、その卓越した成長速度やCO_2吸収量、また鉄に比することのできる材料強度や軽量性から、21世紀のグリーンスチールと呼ぶにふさわしい。建材として使用される樹木が成長するのに最低10年はかかるのに対し、バンブーはたった3年で使用可能になる。換言すれば、木材の代わりにバンブーを使えば森林への負荷をかなり減らすことができる。私たちのバンブー建築には伝統的な構法がいくつか応用されているが、だからといって、私たちの目的がローカルな工芸品を生産することだと思わないで欲しい。私たちが目指しているものは、今日にも通用するサステイナブルな建築であり、そのためにはバンブー建築の生産や建設をシステム化することが肝要である。

私たちの地球はすでに摩耗している。大規模な森林伐採や狂騒的な都市化に歯止めをかけなければならない。明日の建築は、ただ環境への負荷を最小化するに留まらず、自然環境を再生産するものでなければならない。森林の再生に寄与するバンブー建築は、その一翼を担うものであると思っている。

Wind and Water Bar
ウィンド・アンド・ウォーター・バー

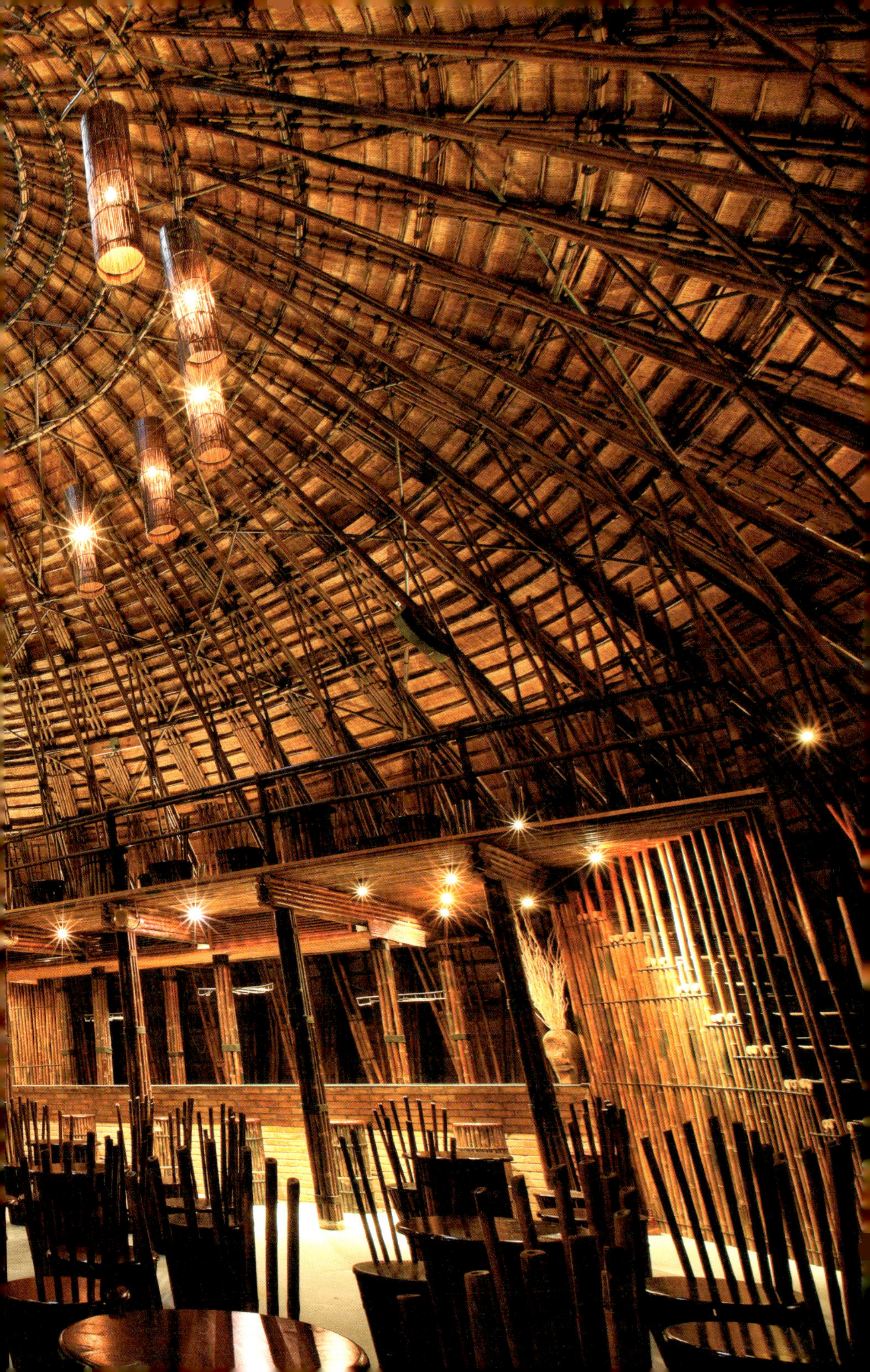

The Wind and Water Bar is a pure bamboo structure located on an artificial pond. Air is cooled by the water of the pond before it flows through the building. The dome structure has been designed by revolving an arch 10 meters tall and 15 meters wide. It consists of 48 "prefabricated" units, and each unit is composed of several bamboo members that have been bound together with rope without using any metal fixtures such as nails. A skylight, 1.5 meters in diameter, has been positioned at the top of the dome for warm air to escape. This dome was our first experiment with systematized bamboo construction and it was built by local workers in 3 months.

「ウィンド・アンド・ウォーター・バー」は、バンブーのみを構造体に用いたプロジェクトである。周囲を水盤に囲まれながら、建物の内部には、水面によって冷やされたそよ風が吹き抜ける。ドーム形状の構造体は、10mの高さと15mのスパンをもつアーチの回転体として構成されており、48の「プレファブ化」されたユニットから成っている。それらのユニットは複数のバンブーをロープで束ねることによってつくられており、その際鉄釘等の金物は一切使用していない。頂部に据えられた直径1.5mのトップライトは、温まった空気の自然排気を促す。このドームはシステム化されたバンブー構造の最初の実験であり、地元の職人によって3か月で建設された。

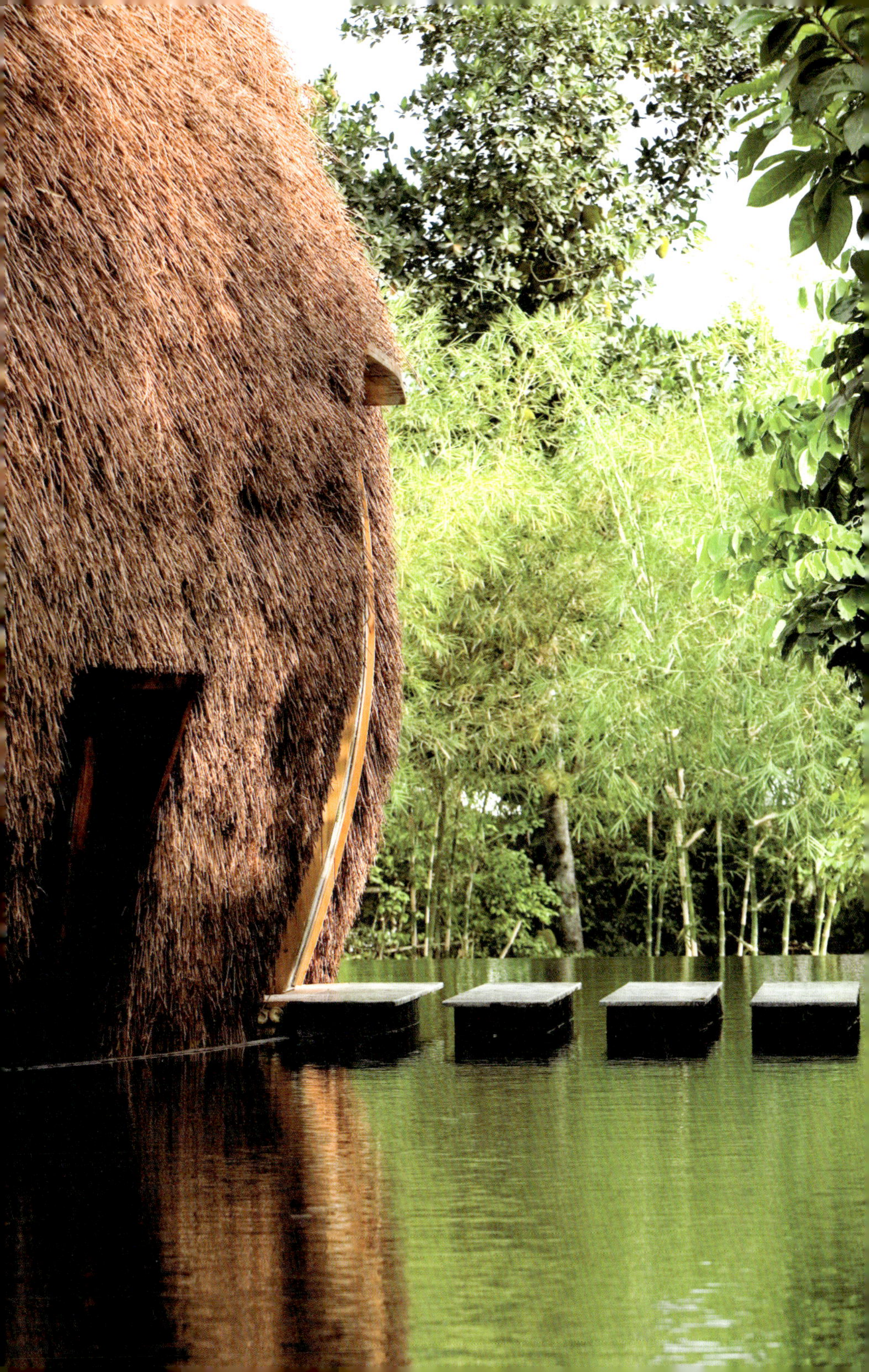

Bamboo Wing
バンブー・ウィング

Surrounded by nature, the Bamboo Wing is a café characterized by its cantilevered structure that is shaped like the wings of a bird flying in the sky. The 12-meter-wide structure is balanced like a scale, supporting a large roof without planting any excessive columns along its perimeter. The airy space that is open to nature is used not only as a café, but also as a venue for the cultural center's conferences, fashion shows, and musical performances. The form of the roof is designed to intake cool wind from the surrounding pond. Additionally, the deep roof blocks the tropical sun and creates a space that can be used comfortably without air conditioning. The volume that houses the kitchen, storage room, and restrooms has been covered entirely with greenery to appear as a hill that blends into the landscape.

「バンブー・ウィング」は自然の中に建つカフェであり、大空を羽ばたく翼のような形状のキャンティレバー構造が特徴である。天秤のように釣り合った全長12mの構造体は、建物外周部に余分な柱を落とすことなく、大きな屋根を支えている。自然に対して開放されたこの空間は、カフェとしてのほか、文化センター主催の会議やファッションショー、音楽のステージとしても利用されている。屋根の形状は、周囲の池から涼しい風を引き込むように設計されている。また、屋根の深さが熱帯の日射しを遮り、空調を使うことなく快適に使用できる空間が生み出されている。キッチン、倉庫、トイレのヴォリュームには全面的な屋上緑化が施されており、周囲の景観に溶け込む丘のようになっている。

Son La Restaurant
ソンラ・レストラン

The Son La Restaurant is located in northern Vietnam and was built using local stone, bamboo, and thatch. In consideration of the tropical monsoon climate, the building is composed of eight stone boxes positioned around an open dining hall. The voids between each box allow for cross ventilation through the interior space. Ninety-six bamboo columns, each composed of four bamboo members, create a forest-like scene of straight bamboo trees inside the hall. The roof is made of local thatch called "vot" that has been overlaid with translucent plastic sheeting. The skylights set between the columns fill the space beneath the roof with a soft light.

「ソンラ・レストラン」はベトナム北部に位置し、現地で調達された石とバンブー、藁を利用して建てられている。熱帯モンスーンの気候に順応するように、8つの石積みの箱が、開放的なダイニングホールを取り囲むように設計されている。箱が分散配置されることによって、建物内部の通風が確保される。ホールでは、4本のバンブーによって構成された96の柱が、垂直に伸びる竹林のような景色をつくり出している。全体を覆う屋根は、現地で「ボット」と呼ばれる藁材の上に半透明のプラスチックシートを被せることで作られている。柱の間に置かれたトップライトが、屋根の下の空間に柔らかい光を導いている。

Milan Expo Pavilion
ミラノ万博パヴィリオン

The Milan Expo Vietnam Pavilion aims to make a forest that provides comfortable shade by planting 46 trees above the building on a site of limited area. The design directly expresses our interest in bringing trees back into the city so that we can live in harmony with nature. The trees are not only visually striking and exciting; they also serve the practical role of blocking solar radiation by casting shadows over the building. The surrounding pool and trees generate a refreshing breeze that cools the entire building, and this greatly contributes to saving energy.

「ミラノ万博パヴィリオン」では、限られた敷地の中に46本の樹木を植え、建物の上に心地良い木陰を落とす森をつくり出そうと試みている。このデザインは、都市に木々を取り戻し、自然との共存を再構築しようという、私たちの方針を表現している。ここに植えられた木々は、見た目の新鮮さや高揚感を与えるに留まらず、日射しを遮り日陰を建物全体に落とすという実際的な役割も果たしている。周囲の水盤と木立は心地よい風を生み、建物全体を涼しくする。これらが一体となり、建物の省エネルギーな運用に大きく寄与している。

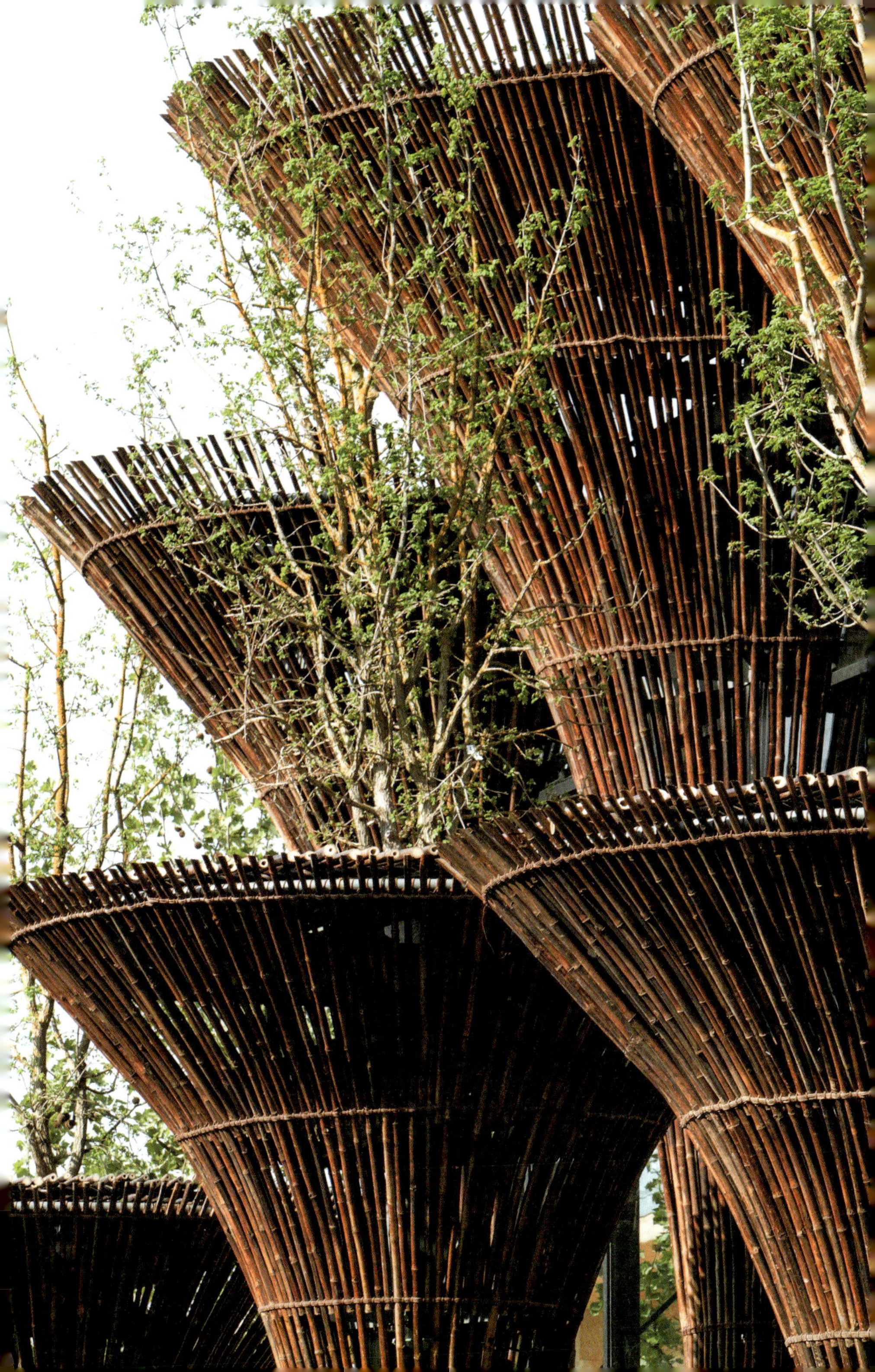

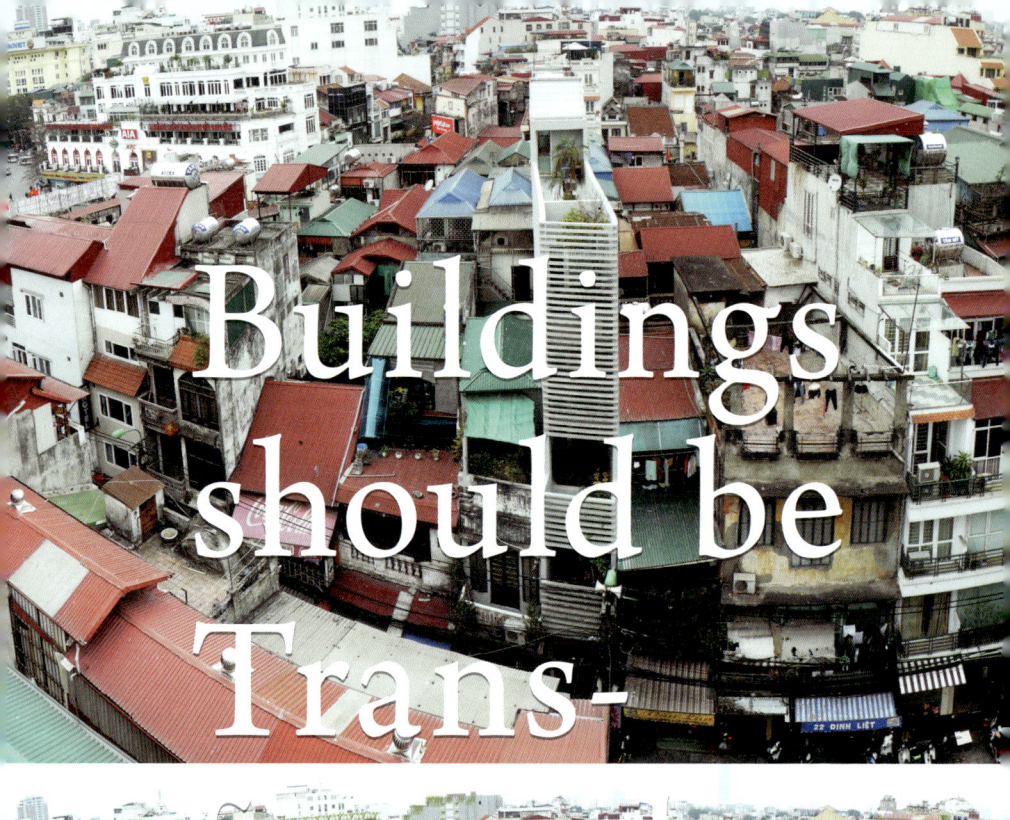

Buildings should be Transformed to house Greenery

We cannot stop people from pursuing a more prosperous life nor stop rapid urbanization. However, if we continue to carry out development in the way that we have been doing, our planet will surely undergo irreversible changes. As architects of this age, our most important duty is to restore greenery on Earth. Architects have the ability to contribute to this task differently from ecologists' approach of defending the environment, namely by designing and planting greenery wherever possible on buildings, such as roofs and facades. If "greened" successfully, a tall building can increase a site's green surface area by more than tenfold. The tower typology that developed out of the 20th century metropolis was originally designed to expand the realm for human activities; today it should be transformed to accommodate greenery. There is a long history of people living in harmony with nature in tropical countries like Vietnam, which have developed their culture and spirit around rich forests. Such countries therefore have great potential to initiate a green architecture movement. We believe that green architecture can actively create a situation where people live in harmony with the earth.

In developing nations that suffer from chronic power shortages, there is a need for buildings that can function with less energy. By observing the world, you will notice that other regions are also facing energy problems, such as the exhaustion of oil and the risks of nuclear power. In this sense, our activities are by no means limited to our specific context. What we must do today is plant more trees than ever before. We will continue to design green architecture with the hope that it will become commonplace everywhere in the world.

人びとが豊かな生活を追い求めるのを止めることはできないし、急速な都市化を止めることもできない。しかし従来の開発を続けるならば、私たちの地球は取り返しのつかない変化を被るだろう。この時代の建築家として、私たちの最大の責務は地球に緑を取り戻すことである。建築家は、生態学者が環境保護を叫ぶ以上のやり方で、この問題に貢献することができる。すなわち屋根やファサード等、建物の至るところに緑をデザインして植えるのである。

もし高層ビルが大規模に緑化されたなら、緑地の面積は敷地の何十倍にも増大する。20世紀の大都市で発展したタワーというタイポロジーは、もともと人間の活動領域を拡大するために生まれたが、いまやそれは緑の容れ物として捉えられるべきである。ベトナムのような熱帯の国々には、自然と共存してきた長い歴史があり、その文化や精神は豊かな森林の周りで育まれてきた。それゆえグリーン建築の運動を起こすのに、熱帯の国々は大きな可能性を秘めている。そしてグリーン建築は、地球が人間と調和して生きていく状況を積極的につくり出すものであると私たちは信じている。

開発途上国においては、慢性的な電力不足のために、より少ないエネルギーで機能する建築が必要とされている。しかし世界の他の地域に目をやっても、石油の枯渇や核エネルギーの危険といったエネルギー問題が、各地で起こっていることに気付くだろう。私たちの活動はその意味で、特殊な地域の特殊な試みに過ぎないわけではない。今日の私たちがすべきことは、昨日よりも多くの木を植えることである。やがてそれが世界の当たり前の風景となる日を目指して、私たちはグリーン建築を設計し続ける。

Stacking Green
スタッキング・グリーン

Stacking Green is a house designed for a couple in their thirties and their mother. It is a row house that stands on a typical narrow plot, measuring 4 meters wide and 20 meters deep. The front and back facades are composed of stacked concrete planters that are cantilevered from the sidewalls. Irrigation pipes have been installed inside the planters to water the plants. The green facade and roof garden protect the inhabitants from direct sunlight and the noise of the street. Skylights, which are a common feature in traditional row houses, provide soft natural lighting that reaches deep into the interior. A cool breeze passes through the house from the porous green facade to the skylights and contributes to minimizing energy consumption.

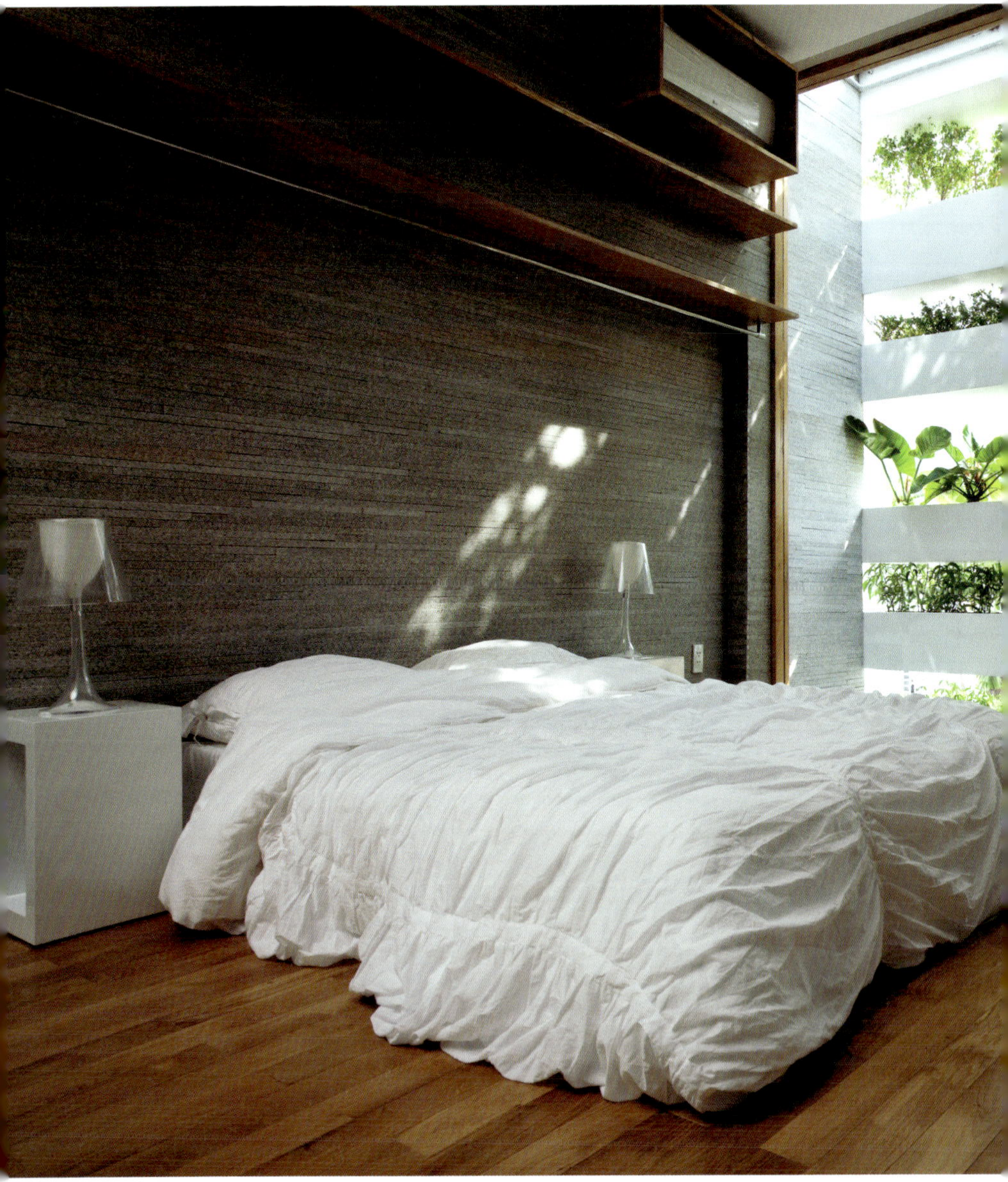

「スタッキング・グリーン」と名付けられたこの住宅は、30代の夫婦と母親のために設計された。幅4m×奥行き20mという典型的な細長い土地に建つ長屋である。前面と背面のファサードは、側壁から張り出したコンクリート製のプランターを積み重ねることで構成している。メンテナンスのための給水パイプは、プランター内部に搭載されている。緑化されたファサードと屋上庭園は、住宅を直射日光や街路の騒音から遠ざけるのに寄与している。伝統的な長屋にも見られるトップライトは、深い室内に柔らかな光を導く。住宅内ではグリーン・ファサードからトップライトへと涼しい風が抜け、エネルギーの消費量は最小限に抑えられている。

House for Trees
ハウス・フォー・ツリー

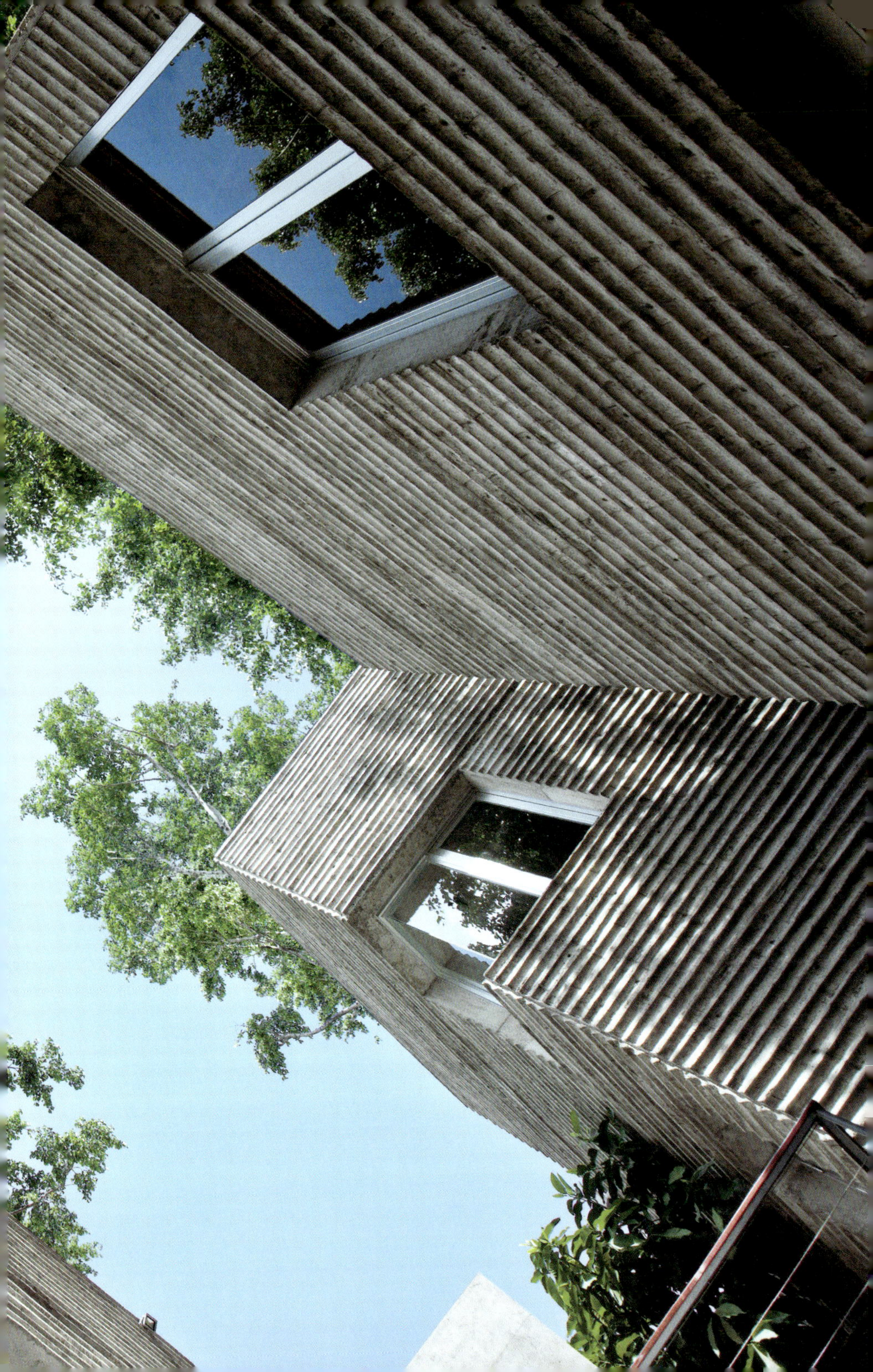

House for Trees is a single-family home located in an area of Ho Chi Minh City where many small houses stand crowded together. The function of this house is divided into five concrete volumes. These volumes are designed as urban greening devices, and they appear as pots with trees planted on top of them. Small gardens occupy the gaps between the volumes and allow the residents to feel the greenery from anywhere in the house. The volumes are connected by steel roofs that create semi-outdoor spaces. The rooftop trees will grow to make "green eaves" in the future. The interior rooms, semi-outdoor spaces, and gardens shaded by the trees, all serve as living spaces for the residents. This is an experimental house that produces a lifestyle in which the line between the inside and outside is blurred appropriately for the tropical climate.

「ハウス・フォー・ツリー」は、小さな住宅がひしめき合うホーチミン市の一角に佇む、ひと家族のために建てられた住宅である。この住宅の機能は、5つのコンクリートの箱に収まっている。箱はいわば都市の緑化装置であり、鉢植えのごとくその上部には大きな木が乗っかっている。箱の隙間もまた小さな庭になっており、住人がどこからでも緑を感じることのできるようになっている。それぞれの箱は鉄板の庇でつながっており、そこが半屋外空間をとなる。将来は屋上の木々が成長し、大きな「緑の庇」をつくるだろう。室内、庇下空間、そして木々の影が落ちる中庭は、そのすべてが生活の場所となり得る。熱帯気候にふさわしい、内外が入り混じったライフスタイルをつくり出す試みである。

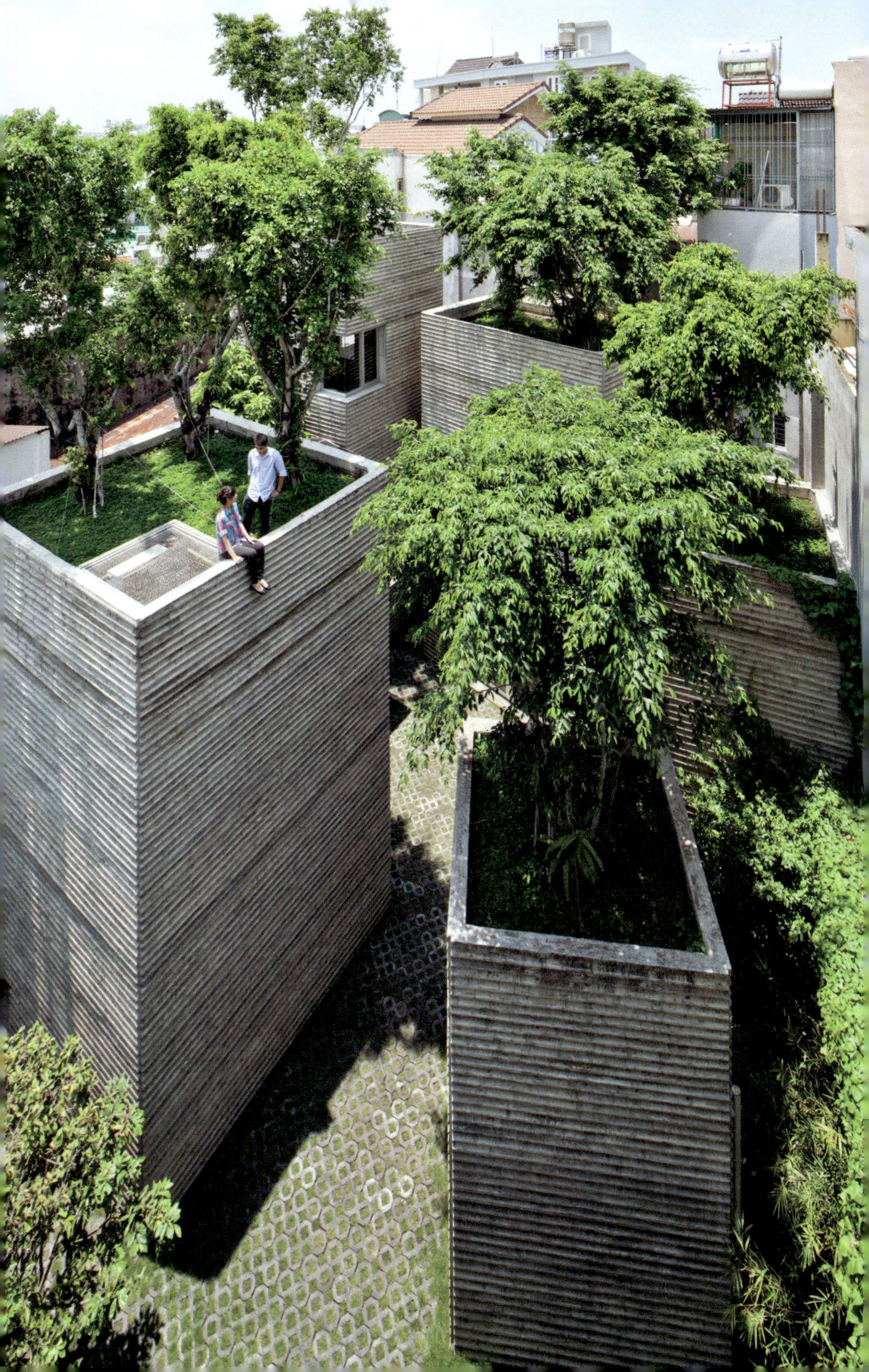

Farming Kindergarten
ファーミング・キンダーガーテン

The Farming Kindergarten is a kindergarten for 500 children. It is a prototype for a sustainable education space in a tropical climate. The building is used by the children of the workers of the adjacent factory. The building concept is to create a continuous green roof that provides vegetables and agricultural learning experiences for the Vietnamese children. The green roof forms a continuous loop with three rings that create three courtyards. The courtyards serve as safe and comfortable playgrounds for the children. Both ends of the roof slope down to meet the courtyard, giving the children the special experience of walking up and along the green roof. The roof is a continuous vegetable garden and provides a place for children to learn about agriculture and the importance of our relationship with nature.

「ファーミング・キンダーガーテン」は500人の未就学児が集う幼稚園である。熱帯におけるサステイナブルな教育空間のプロトタイプとして、隣接する工場の、作業員の子供たちのために使用されている。建物のコンセプトは、ベトナムの子供に野菜と農業体験をもたらす、連続的な緑の屋根を作り出すことである。緑化された屋根はひと筆描きの3重の輪を形づくり、内側に3つの中庭を囲い込む。中庭は、安全で快適な子供たちの遊び場となる。屋根の両端は中庭に滑りこむように接地しており、子供たちはこの屋根に上り、歩き回ることで、特別なかたちで自然に親しむことを体験する。屋根は連続的な菜園として設計されており、子供たちに農業と自然との関わりの大切さを教える場になっている。

115

Wind and Water Café
ウィンド・アンド・ウォーター・カフェ

Shanghai Expo Vietnam Pavilion
上海万博ベトナム・パヴィリオン

Founded in 2006, Vo Trong Nghia Architects is a leading architectural practice in Vietnam. More than 60 architects, engineers, and support staff work together on cultural, commercial, and residential projects worldwide out of offices in Ho Chi Minh City and Hanoi.

We have been exploring new methods for creating sustainable architecture for the 21st century while maintaining the essence of Asian architecture. In the rapidly developing nation of Vietnam, it is vital that we utilize renewable energy, employ local materials, and create architecture with spaces and expressions that project a new vision of Vietnam. We understand that it is this kind of architecture that will be acknowledged by the world.

Our bamboo projects show that they can meet the demands of the contemporary age. Bamboo tends not to be used as the main structural material of buildings because it is difficult to handle compared to timber, but bamboo has been receiving attention for its strength and its ability to grow rapidly. Bamboo can be found in almost all regions of tropical Asia, and it allows for cheaper construction compared to other building materials. We have organized our own team of specialists in bamboo construction to overcome the technical issues of building bamboo architecture.

Our green projects are driven by our awareness of a rather pressing problem. The amount of greenery lost in Vietnam over these past few decades is immeasurable. Our ultimate goal is to slow, and hopefully reverse, the ongoing decline of our planet's green areas. Individual buildings may not have the power to do this. However, it may be possible for us to make a large impact on society by guiding Vietnam's architectural community with our collective body of green buildings. We believe that our activities are becoming more significant every day in Vietnam where the concept of architecture is now finally taking shape.

Binh Duong School
ビンズン・スクール

Binh Thanh House
ビンタン・ハウス

Dai Lai Conference Hall
ダイライ・コンファレンス・ホール

Kon Tum Indochine Café
コントゥム・インドシン・カフェ

2006年に設立されたヴォ・チョン・ギア・アーキテクツは、ベトナム建築界をリードする設計事務所である。ホーチミンシティとハノイにおいて、総勢60人を超える建築家、エンジニア、その他関連スタッフが、文化施設や商業施設、住宅など多岐にわたる国内外のプロジェクトに携わっている。

アジア建築のエッセンスを尊重した上で、私たちは21世紀のサステイナブルな建築を生み出す、新たな方法を模索している。自然エネルギーを採り入れ、ローカルな材料を活用し、かつ建築の表現や空間はベトナムにおける新たなヴィジョンを指し示していること。このいずれもが、急速な発展によって、ますます重要な局面を迎えつつあるこの国には必要だし、またそれらを兼ね備えたもののみが世界に認められるということを、私たちは知っている。

私たちの一連のバンブー・プロジェクトは、それらが現代的な要求にも通用するということを示している。バンブーという材料は、その強度や再生能力がにわかに注目されつつも、製材に比べて扱いづらいという理由から、建築の主構造としては敬遠されがちである。しかし、バンブーは熱帯アジアのほぼ全域に自生しており、他の建材に比べ低価格で建設することができる。私たちは専門の職人チームを率いることにより、バンブーを使った建設の技術的な問題を克服している。

グリーン・プロジェクトのほうは、やや切迫した問題意識に駆り立てられている。この数十年の開発で、ベトナムが失った緑の量は計り知れない。今日もなお続く緑地の下降曲線に歯止めをかけ、願わくは上昇に転じるのが、私たちの究極の目標である。個々の建築自体にはその力はないかもしれない。しかしベトナム建築界の先達として、私たちのグリーン建築が全体として社会に影響を与えるということはあり得る。建築という概念がようやく形成されつつあるベトナムにおいては、私たちの活動がもたらす意義は日増しに強まっていると考えている。

Green Renovation
グリーン・リノベーション

Nam An Retreat
ナムアン・リトリート

大西麻貴＋百田有希

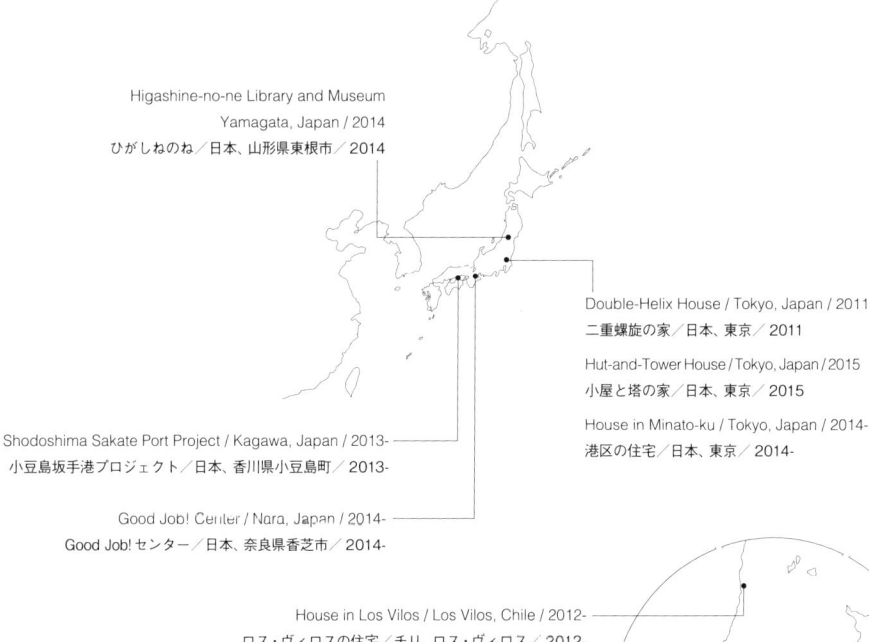

Higashine-no-ne Library and Museum
Yamagata, Japan / 2014
ひがしねのね／日本、山形県東根市／ 2014

Double-Helix House / Tokyo, Japan / 2011
二重螺旋の家／日本、東京／ 2011

Hut-and-Tower House / Tokyo, Japan / 2015
小屋と塔の家／日本、東京／ 2015

House in Minato-ku / Tokyo, Japan / 2014-
港区の住宅／日本、東京／ 2014-

Shodoshima Sakate Port Project / Kagawa, Japan / 2013-
小豆島坂手港プロジェクト／日本、香川県小豆島町／ 2013-

Good Job! Center / Nara, Japan / 2014-
Good Job! センター／日本、奈良県香芝市／ 2014-

House in Los Vilos / Los Vilos, Chile / 2012-
ロス・ヴィロスの住宅／チリ、ロス・ヴィロス／ 2012-

Maki ONISHI +Yuki HYAKUDA

Introductory Essay / Erwin Viray

The initial impression of o+h is the relationship of the studio to the street and the interior space, the operation of making architecture can be seen from the street, and from inside the street life can be seen too. It is spectacle, an openness creating a dialogue with the public and with the community. This attitude is an expression of the pursuits of o+h, the exploration on a path, a research on circulation, the perception of a place, an unfolding, the surprise of discovery, the life of an everyday, an experiment of exploring the boundaries of public and private. It is the movement in space that makes us aware of our body and our perceptions, our existence and the relationship to our environment. As we move and stop to make a pause, we encounter certain highlights that we normally have taken for granted. The o+h approach is a vision that engages the user and the public to full participation in appreciating a place beyond architectural form opening a path to developing potentials of the architect in shifting times, specially in Japan clothed with uncertainly, like now.

紹介文／エルウィン・ビライ

　o+hについて最初に印象深かったことは、スタジオと通りとの関係で、内部の建築をつくっているのが通りから見えることである。反対に中からも通りの生活を見ることができる。それは見もので、このあけっぴろげなところが、ひとびととそしてコミュニティとの対話をつくり出す。この姿勢がo+hの追求していることの、ひとつの表明である。小径の探検、サーキュレーションのリサーチ、場所の認識、展開すること、驚きの発見、日常の生活、公と私の境い目を探る実験。それはわれわれの身体や意識、われわれの存在、周囲との関係をわれわれに気付かせる、空間における運動である。動いた時や一拍休む時、われわれは通常当たり前のように考えている、ある印象的な瞬間に出会う。o+hのアプローチは、ユーザーや一般の人に、建築的な形態を超えた、場所の価値に気付く作業に参加してもらい、建築家のポテンシャルを拡げる道をつけるという展望である。特に不確実さで覆われた今の日本において。

経験の一部としての建築
Architecture as Part of an Experience

まちから建築へ、建築からまちへとひとつながりに続く建築について考えたい。人が建築を体験する時、その体験はすでにまちから始まっている。
どのような道を歩き、誰と出会い、何を感じたか。
どのようにアプローチして、どのように出て行ったか。
そういった経験全体の一部として建築を考えることで、敷地での佇まいや、中と外の関係、空間そのもののつくられ方がおのずとその土地にとって自然なものとして設計できるのではないかと考えている。

We think architecture should be one continuous experience
-from town to architecture and from architecture to town.
When we encounter a piece of architecture, the experience begins before we even enter the building.
Which path we chose that led us there, who we met along the way, what emotions we felt.
How we approach it, and how we exit this piece of architecture.
When we consider architecture as a part of this whole experience, the way the building is positioned on its site, the relationship between the exterior and interior, and the creation of the space itself should all fall into place. A piece of architecture that responds naturally to its townscape will be made possible.

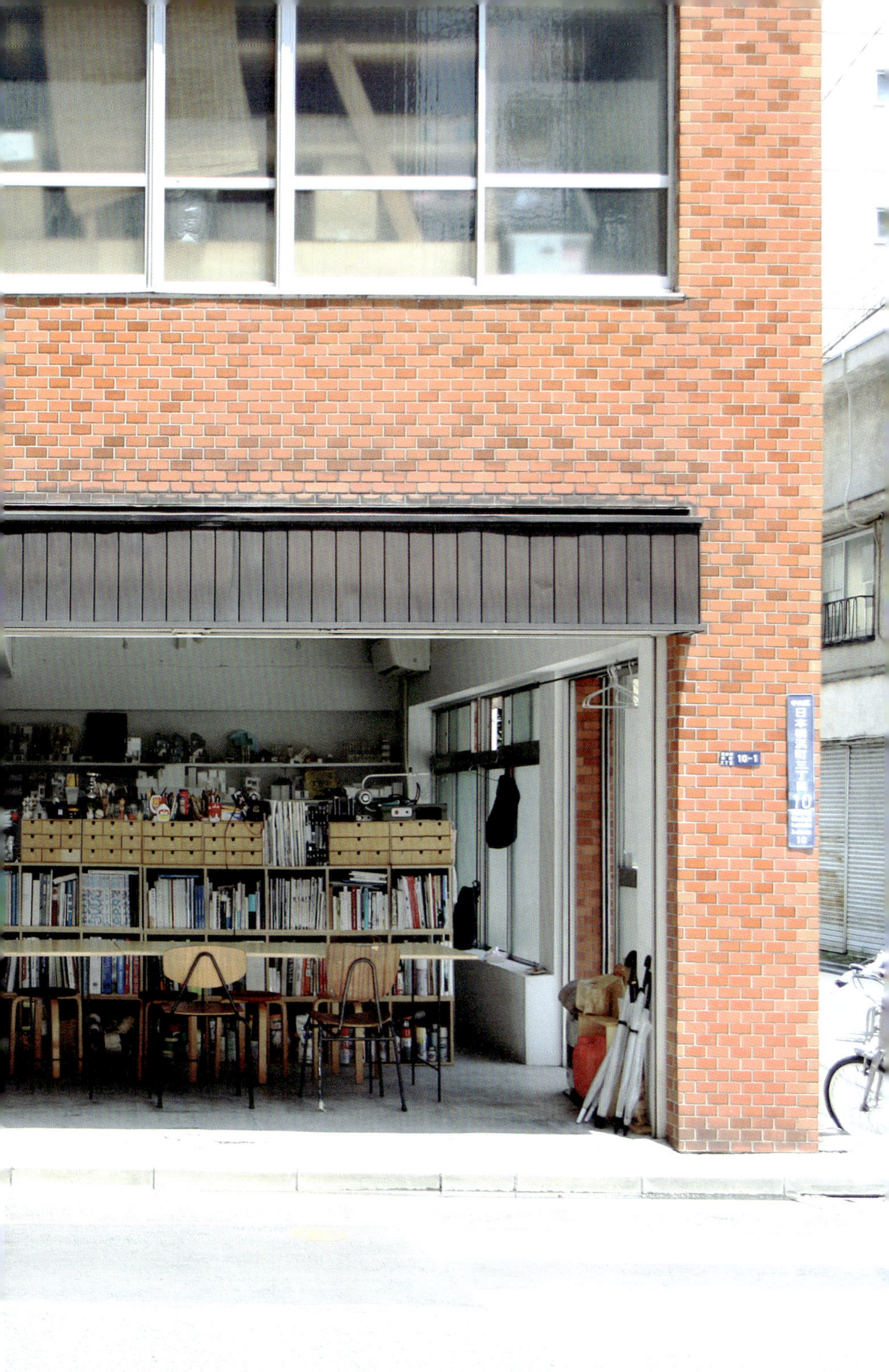

倉庫
Storage

道路と連続するミーティング兼模型作業スペース
Meeting space/model-making space continuous with the street

道路でキャッチボール
Playing catch in the street

事務所の様子
Views of the office

プライベートなパソコン作業スペース
Private space for computer work

私たちの事務所は、日本橋浜町という江戸の気質が残る東京の下町にある。道路に面した1階で、もともとガレージだった所を使っている。引っ越してもうすぐ1年になるのだが、入り口にはまだシャッターしか付いていない。だから、毎日八百屋のように通りに開け放たれた状態になっている。そうすると、ホコリがすごかったり、水道工事が始まるとうるさくて打ち合わせどころではなかったりといろいろ大変なことがあるのだが、まちとの距離が近くなって、近所の方が手作りのお菓子を差し入れてくださったり、子供たちがふらっと遊びに来たり、面白いこともたくさんある。私たち自身のまちに対する態度をほんの少し変えるだけで、こんなにもまちとの楽しく豊かな関係が始まるのだなといつも驚かされている。

Our office is located in Nihonbashi Hamacho, which is a low-lying neighborhood of Tokyo that still retains the old Edo atmosphere. Formerly a garage, the space that we are using is on the ground floor and faces a street. It has been nearly a year since we moved here, but the entrance is still only equipped with a roller shutter. We therefore always leave it left wide open to the street in the same manner as a vegetable shop. This causes many inconveniences, such as the large amount of dust that comes inside and the noise of construction work on the waterworks that prevents us from holding meetings. However, it also brings us closer to the city and invites many interesting things to happen. For example, neighbors will bring us homemade snacks and children will wander inside to play. We are constantly surprised by how we have been able to initiate such a fun and rich relationship with the city just by making this small change in our attitude toward the street.

二重螺旋の家
Double-Helix House

東京都谷中にある、夫婦と3人の子供たちのための家。
A house for a couple and their three children in Yanaka, Tokyo.

この家は、中心の白く四角い部屋に、細長い廊下が巻き付くという単純な構成で出来ている。廊下は幅が広くなったり、傾斜が緩やかになったりすることで、小さな図書スペースになったり、子供の遊び場になったりする。

The house's configuration is simple: a core of square white rooms with a long narrow corridor winding around it. The corridor widens or levels off in places to form a small library and play area for the children.

onishimaki+hyakudayuki / o+h 127

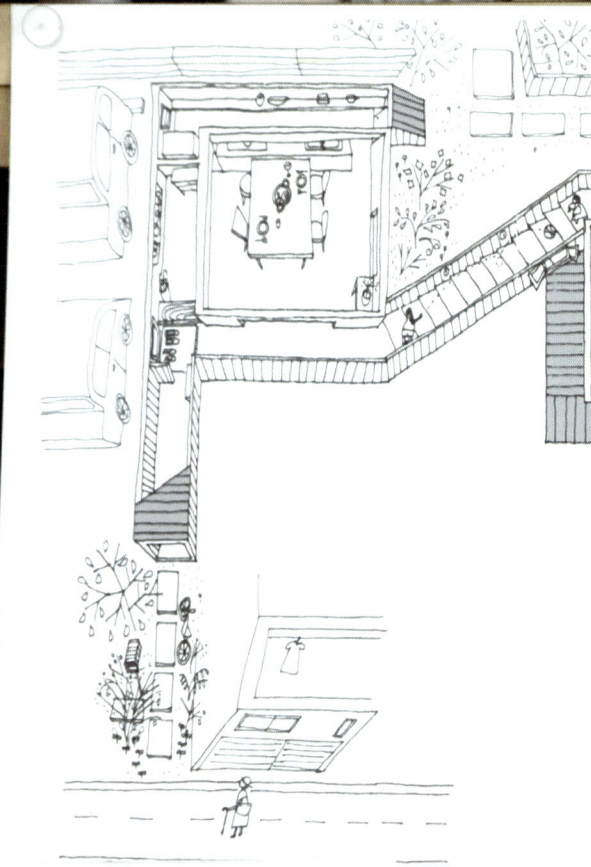

この家にははっきりとした玄関がない。路地を歩いていると、いつのまにか半屋外の廊下が始まるので、どこまでがまちでどこからが家か、経験の上で曖昧である。また、屋内と屋外の両方に階段が付いているのでどこまで行っても行き止まりのない、体験の長い住宅となった。

This house does not have a clear entrance. The semi-outdoor corridor begins abruptly as one walks along the alley, so as an experience it is ambiguous where the city ends and where the house begins. Furthermore, the house offers an extended experience because there are stairs on both the inside and outside that never lead to a dead end.

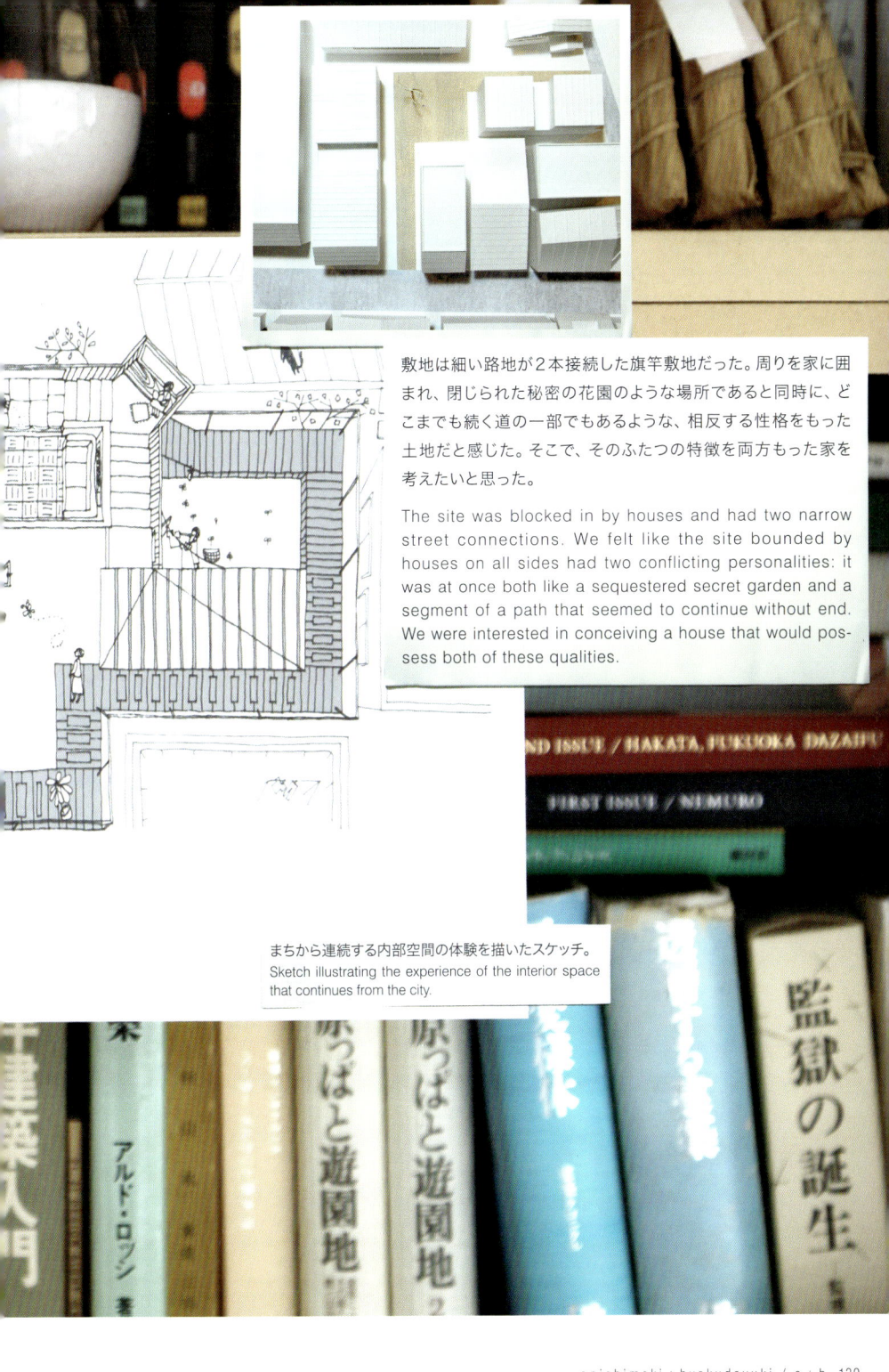

敷地は細い路地が2本接続した旗竿敷地だった。周りを家に囲まれ、閉じられた秘密の花園のような場所であると同時に、どこまでも続く道の一部でもあるような、相反する性格をもった土地だと感じた。そこで、そのふたつの特徴を両方もった家を考えたいと思った。

The site was blocked in by houses and had two narrow street connections. We felt like the site bounded by houses on all sides had two conflicting personalities: it was at once both like a sequestered secret garden and a segment of a path that seemed to continue without end. We were interested in conceiving a house that would possess both of these qualities.

まちから連続する内部空間の体験を描いたスケッチ。
Sketch illustrating the experience of the interior space that continues from the city.

小豆島 坂手港 プロジェクト
Shodoshima Sakate Port Project

小豆島の関西方面からの玄関港、坂手のまち全体の未来について考えるプロジェクト。

A project for thinking about the future of the entire town of Sakate, the port of entry to Shodoshima for travelers from the Kansai region.

まちと外をつなぐ場所としてのエリエス荘　2014年春〜
The Elies Lodge as a Place for Connecting the Town with the Outside World Spring 2014–

瀬戸内国際芸術祭期間中、多くのクリエイターが宿泊した元町営宿泊施設「エリエス荘」の建て替え計画。期間中、1階の食堂ではクリエイターとまちの人が集まり、毎日のように飲み会が開催された。

A plan to build a new Elies Lodge, a former municipal lodging facility where many creators stayed during the Setouchi International Art Festival. Creators and local residents held get-togethers in the cafeteria on the first floor almost every day during the event.

深い窓辺がベッドになる。宿泊者が少ない時には海を見るベンチとなる。

The deep spaces beside the windows become beds. They serve as benches for looking out to the sea when there are not many guests.

小豆島の玄関としての港の計画　2014年夏〜
Plan of the Port as an Entrance to Shodoshima Summer 2014–

11日間の滞在から　2013年夏
From an 11-Day Stay Summer 2013

瀬戸内国際芸術祭期間中に、クリエイター・イン・レジデンスとして11日間坂手港に滞在し、地元の中学生のゆうこちゃんと一緒に10年後の坂手の未来を考えるワークショップを行った。

We stayed in Sakate Port for 11 days as creators in residence during the Setouchi International Art Festival and held workshops to think about Sakate's future in 10 years together with Yuko-chan, a local middle-school student.

ワークショップを通して教えてもらったまちのさまざまなルートと、それにまつわる記憶を、経験ごとにひとつながりの地図にまとめたもの。

We compiled a map showing the various routes through the town and the memories associated with them for each experience that we learnt about in the workshops.

空地の夕暮れ演奏会　2013年夏
Evening Concert in a Vacant Lot Summer 2013

ワークショップで教えてもらった迷路のようなまちの魅力を、みんなで体感するために小豆島高校ブラスバンド部協力のもと、空地を使った演奏会を行った。

We held a concert in a vacant lot with the help of the Shodoshima High School's brass band club so that everyone could experience the appeal of the town's maze-like character that we learned about in the workshops.

坂手の未来をスケッチで描く　2014年春
Drawing Sketches of Sakate's Future Spring 2014

坂手に通いながら伺ったお話やワークショップを元に、まちの未来についてスケッチを描いた。玄関港としての埠頭と産直市場、新しいエリエス荘（宿泊施設）、商店街の新しい使われ方、空地を使った共同の水場、子育てと高齢者の集まる場所などのイメージが含まれる。

We drew sketches of Sakate's future based on the workshops and conversations that we held during our visits to the town. They include renderings of the wharf as an entry port, a local produce market, a new Elies Lodge (lodging facility), the shopping street being used in new ways, a common water park made by utilizing a vacant lot, and a place for child-raising parents and elderly residents to gather together.

暮らしと一体となった福祉　2015年　春〜
Welfare Integrated with Everyday Life Spring 2015–

子供たちからお年寄り、障がいをもつ人まで、皆が慣れ親しんだ地で共に過ごすことのできる場所の計画。元幼稚園を地域のサロンに改修し、その横に小規模多機能施設を設計する。

A plan for a place where children, the elderly, and people with disabilities can be together in their familiar settings. We will remodel the former kindergarten into a community salon and design a small multi-functional group home for multifunctional long-term care next to it.

小屋と塔の家
Hut-and-Tower House

東京都目黒区の、夫婦とふたりの子供たちのための家。
A house for a couple and two children in Meguro, Tokyo.

あちこちにテラスや中庭といった屋外の居場所をもつ家である。内部階段とは別に屋外階段が付いているので、日常生活にちょっと外を通る、という体験が自然と生まれる。そうすることで自分がどんなまちに暮らしているか、今どんな季節なのかということがもっと感じられるのではないかと考えた。

This is a house that has many outdoor spaces, such as terraces and courtyards. It has external stairs in addition to internal stairs, so it naturally invites its residents to step outside in their daily lives. We think that this will make them become more aware of the seasons and of the settings that they live in.

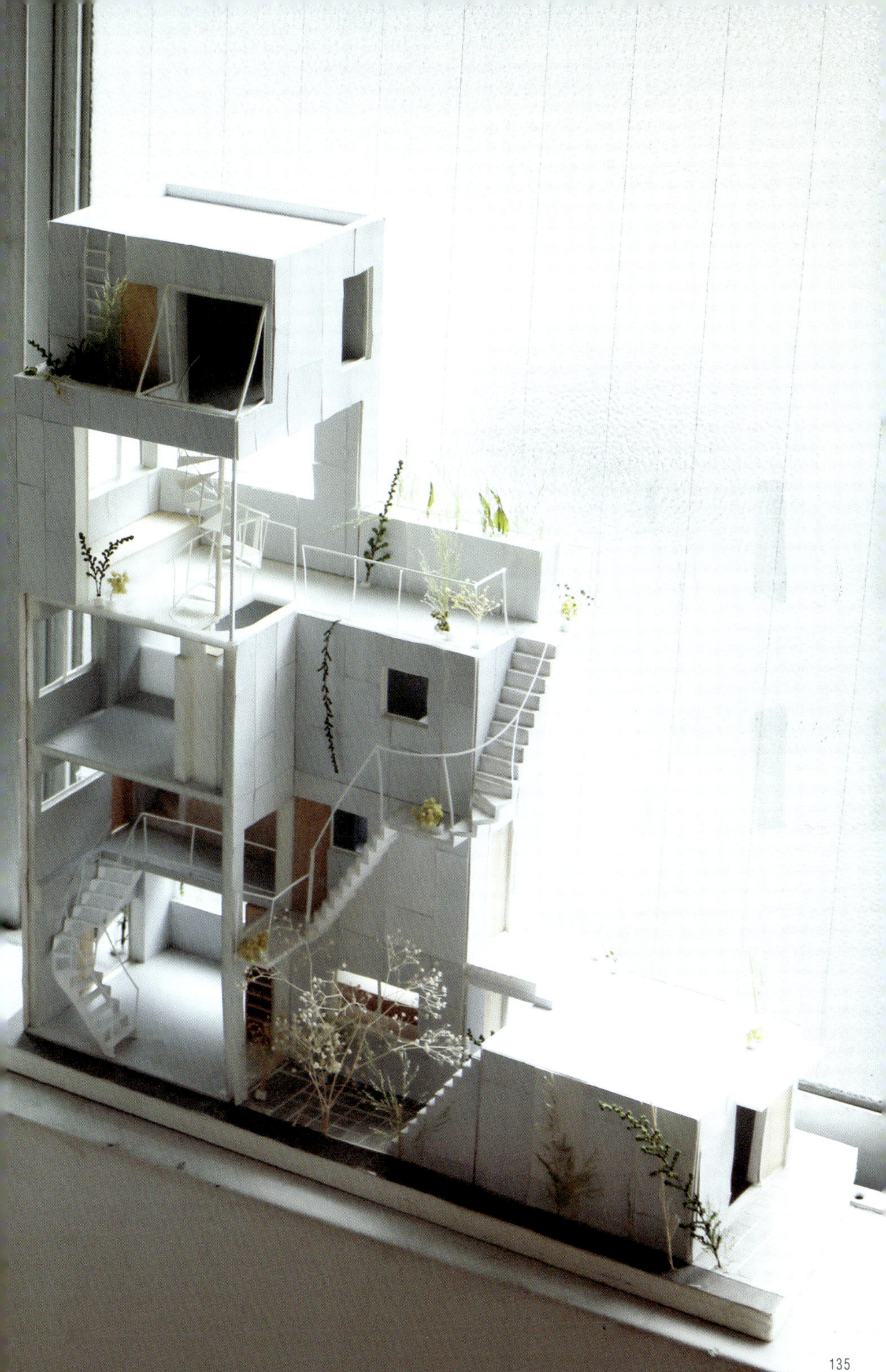

ひがしねのね
Higashine-no-ne Library and Museum

山形県東根市における、図書館と歴史資料館のコンペ提出案。
A competition proposal for a library and history museum in Higashine, Yamagata.

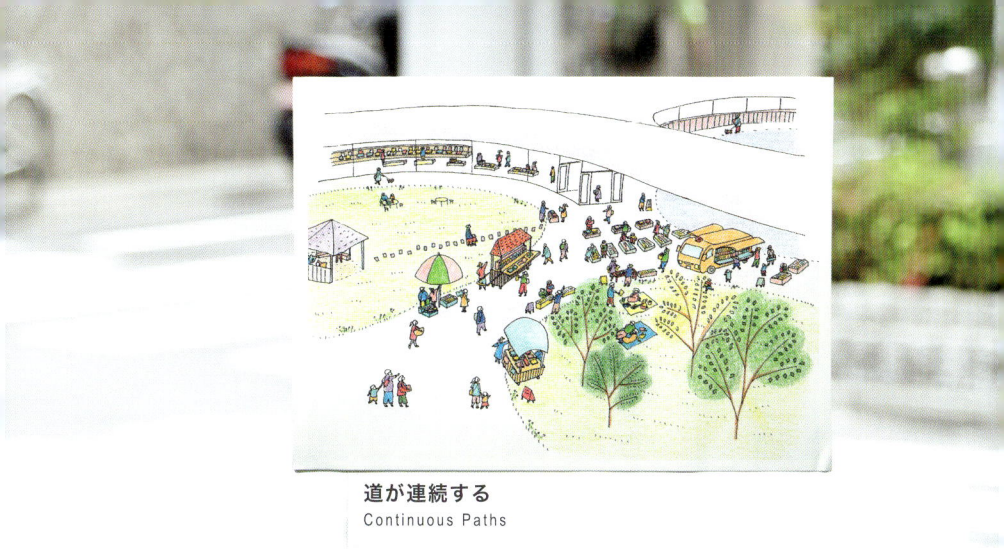

道が連続する
Continuous Paths

まちから続く道が、そのまま中へと連続する建築。図書館や美術館が道からひとつながりに展開し、互いに交差する。何気ない散策の中に思いもよらない出合いが生まれる。

Paths from the city continue directly into the building. The library and museum unfold along paths that intersect with one another. Chance encounters are born as people casually walk about.

GoodJob! センター
GoodJob! Center

GoodJob! センターは奈良県香芝市に計画中の障がいのある方と共に新しい仕事を生み出すための施設である。障がいをもつ人ももたない人も、地元の方も遠方からの来訪者も、それぞれに居場所があり個性を生かしながら共に働くことのできる場所として構想された。

The GoodJob! Center that we are currently designing in Kashiba, Nara, is a facility that aims to create new jobs together with people with disabilities. It is planned to become a place where people with disabilities, people without disabilities, local residents, and visitors from afar can all feel they belong and can work together by capitalizing on their individual traits.

私たちはたくさんの小さな居場所が集まってできたような建築がつくれないかと考えた。例えば広い場所で大きな机を囲んで作業する場所の奥に、静かで落ち着いた窓際があるなど、多様な場面が緩やかにつながってお互いの気配が感じられる空間である。

We have imagined the building as an assemblage of many small places. The spaces loosely connect a variety of scenes and enable people to sense each others' presence. For instance, there is a large open area for people to work together around a big table, while behind it there is a more hushed, restful space beside a window.

まち並みをつくる
Shaping the Streetscape

ふたつの建築を同じ街区のふたつの敷地に建てることで、エリア全体の雰囲気が少し変わるような佇まいを考えている。

Because we are making two buildings on two sites in the same district, we are designing their appearance in a way that might slightly change the atmosphere of the entire area.

壁、床、天井、屋根、家具、照明等がばらばらと場所をつくることで、ここで展開する活動がそのまま建築の佇まいとなって現れるような建築にしたいと考えている。

We want the activities that take place within the building to directly shape its appearance by having the scattered walls, floors, ceilings, roofs, furniture, and lighting define a variety of places.

GoodJob! センター　スタディ過程
GoodJob! Center Study Process

南棟　2014.1
コンペ案。壁柱によって森のような場所をつくる。

South Wing 2014.1
Competition proposal. The columnar walls create a place like a forest.

南棟　2015.1
倉庫に囲まれる案。吹き抜けた2階に一周倉庫を配置した大きなワンルーム。

South Wing 2015.1
Perimeter storage scheme. A single large double-height room with storage positioned along the perimeter of the second floor.

南棟　2015.2
倉庫+ブリッジ案。2階の倉庫を分解し、ブリッジでつなぐ。

South Wing 2015.2
Storage + bridge scheme. The storage is scattered across the second floor and linked by bridges.

南棟　2015.3
ばらばら案。壁、サッシ、家具、屋根等が全てばらばらと集まって居場所をつくる。

South Wing 2015.3
Scattered scheme. The scattered walls, window frames, furniture, roof, etc. define the spaces together.

北棟　2014.1
コンペ案。壁柱によって南棟と連動したまち並みをつくる。

North Wing 2014.1
Competition proposal. Shaping the streetscape by using columnar walls that echo the design of the south wing.

北棟　2014.2
ランドスケープ案。壁柱だけでない、さまざまな要素で公園のような場所をつくる。

North Wing 2014.2
Landscape scheme. Creating a park-like place by using various elements other than just columnar walls.

北棟　2014.7
平屋壁柱案。敷地の傾斜を利用し、平屋ワンルームに壁柱で居場所をつくる。

North Wing 2014.7
Single-story scheme with columnar walls. Defining place with the columnar walls in a one-room single-story volume that makes use of the site's sloping topography.

北棟　2014.4
壁がつながる案。連続したり枝分かれしたりする壁によって、空間を緩やかに仕切る。

North Wing 2014.4
Continuous wall scheme. The continuous wall that branches off in places loosely partitions the spaces.

onishimaki+hyakudayuki / o+h　143

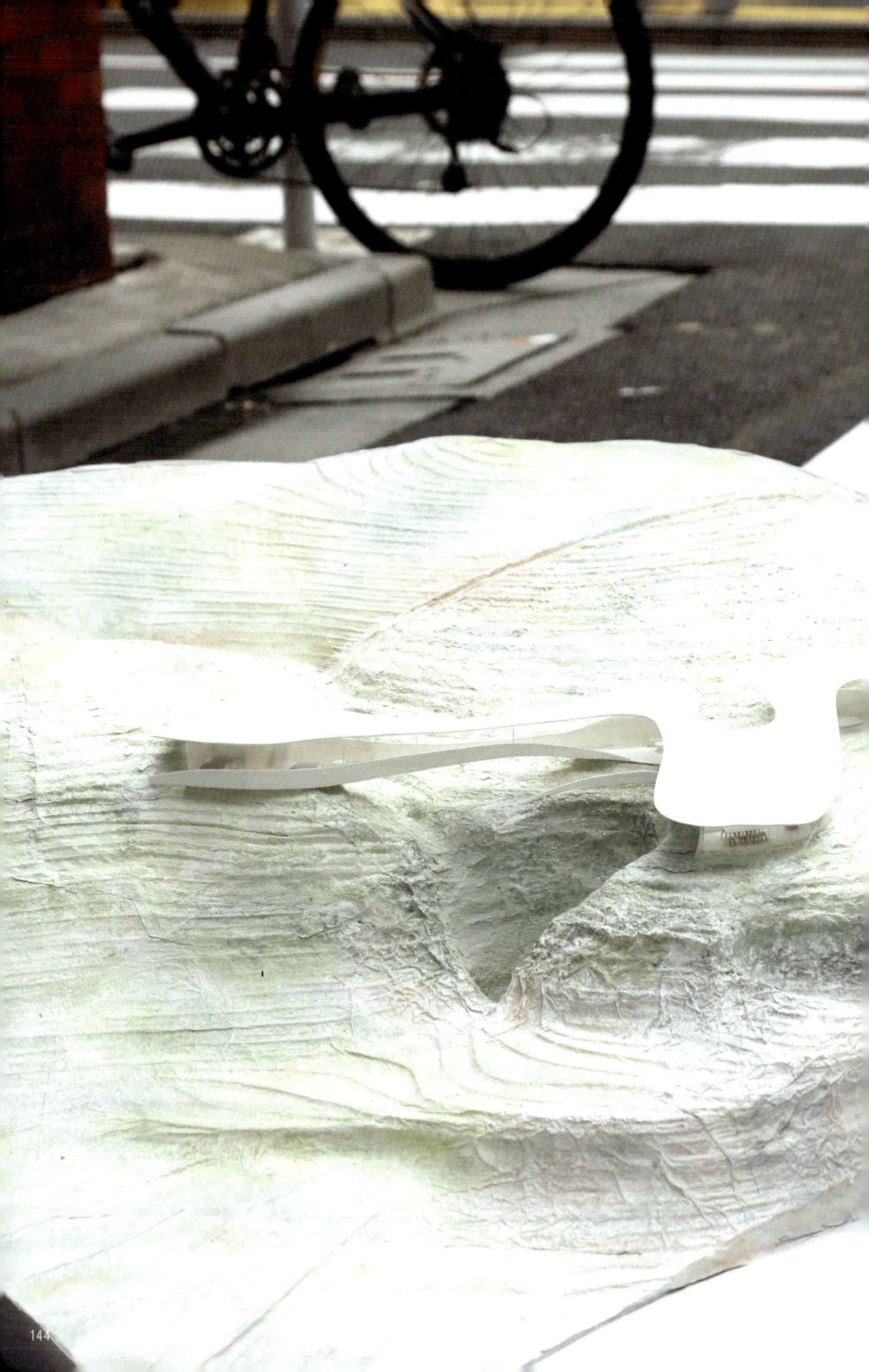

ロス・ヴィロスの住宅
House in Los Vilos

チリのロス・ヴィロスに計画中の週末住宅。太平洋に面した、荒々しく美しい自然の中を歩いてアプローチする体験が、家の中にまで連続する。

A weekend house that we are currently planning in Los Vilos, Chile. The experience of approaching the house by walking through the rough, beautiful nature along the Pacific Ocean continues inside.

港区の住宅
House in Minato-ku

港区に計画中の、夫婦のための小さな住宅。
A small house currently being planned for a couple in Minato-ku.

大きな吹き抜け　2014.10
吹き抜け空間を動く床に乗って移動する案。

Large Atrium 2014.10
Scheme with an atrium traversed by riding on a moving floor.

大きな場所　小さな場所　2014.8
大空間を小さな居場所が取り巻く。

Big Place, Small Place 2014.8
A big space encircled by small niches.

動く床　2014.5
大きさ、明るさの異なる階を動く床が上下する。

Moving Floor 2014.5
A floor moves up and down to levels of varying sizes and brightness.

透明なかたまり　2014.12
壁がぱらぱらと集まった透明な状態。

Transparent Mass 2014.12
A transparent assemblage of scattered walls.

外と中の間　2015.5
部屋の周りをたくさんの半屋外のバルコニーや
テラスが取り巻く。風が通り抜ける家。

Between Outside and Inside 2015.5
Rooms with plenty of semi-outdoor balconies and
terraces. An airy house.

あたたかい建築　2015.3
もっとおおらかな場所の出来方を考える。
匂いや表情の感じられる家。

Warm Architecture 2015.3
Thinking about making place more generously.
A house where one can smell scents and see
expressions.

onishimaki＋hyakudayuki／o+h 147

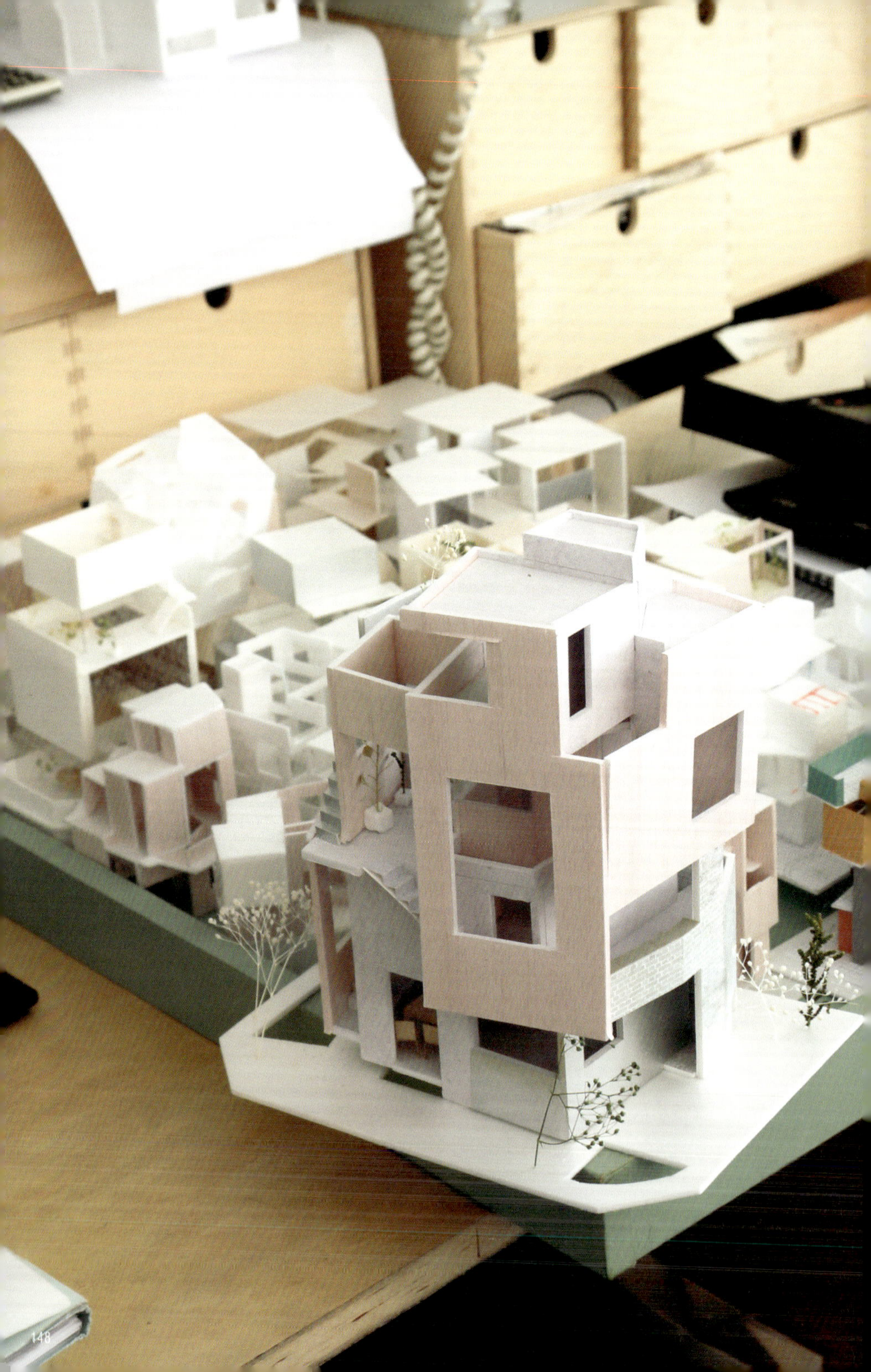

断片的なシーンの積み重ねで全体ができたような、また、全体があってその中にシーンを発見するような、部分と全体のどちらが先にあったか分からないような状態をつくりたい。まるで建築が自分の力で成長していった先で、それぞれの場所に反応して細部のかたちを変え、最終的に得体の知れない状態になるようなイメージである。設計という運動がそのままかたちになったような、勢いと柔軟さをもつ建築を考えてみたい。

We want to create a state in which it is unclear whether the parts or the whole came first, such that it appears as if the whole is made of an accumulation of fragmentary scenes and also as if there is a whole within which the scenes are discovered. We are imagining the building to seem as if it has grown on its own, transformed its details in response to its particular site, and in the end become something that is inexplicable. We want to conceive an architecture that has both momentum and flexibility in a way that it seems as if the form is a direct embodiment of the act of design.

We relocated our office from the fifth floor of an apartment in Meguro to Hamacho after we had worked on projects based in places such as Tohoku, Shodoshima, and Nara, because we realized the great architectural potential of interacting with small towns and their residents. For instance, in the case of Shodoshima, where we are planning several projects for the whole town at Sakate Port, we are developing the designs through a method that differs entirely from the usual approach of visiting the town just for project meetings. We would instead stay in town for long periods of time and revisit it over and over again so that we can drink together with the local residents and update each other on the progress of things. Through these casual conversations, we

愛される建築を目指して
Towards a Cherishable Architecture

　私たちがもともと目黒にあるマンションの５階にあった事務所を浜町へ引っ越したのは、東北や小豆島、奈良などで仕事をするようになって、まちや人と関わりながら建築を考えることに大きな可能性を感じたからだ。例えば、私たちは今小豆島坂手港でまち全体を構想するいくつかのプロジェクトに取り組んでいるが、その際の設計の進め方は建築の打ち合わせをするためだけにまちに通うということとは大きく異なっている。長くまちに滞在し、また何度も通うことで、まちの人びととお酒を一緒に飲んだり、近況を訪ね合ったり、何気ない会話の中で建築をひとつつくること以上のさまざまなことに巻き込まれていく。その体験は私たちの中に少しずつ染み込んでいって、設計をする時にも確実に思い返されている。つまり私たちが建築をイメージする時、その中で活動している人は、ある抽象的な人でもなく、小豆島の人、という漠然とした印象でもない、ゆうこちゃん、久留島さん、谷さん、まさこさんといった生の人間であり、それが同時にまだ会ったことのない、あるいはこれから生まれてきてこの建築と出会う新しい人びとも含むという感覚である。それは特定の人の具体的な要望や意見を聞いてつくるという建築とも少し違った、例えるならば食べ物がいつの間にか自分の血となり肉となるというようなゆっくりとした、しかし確実な私たちの設計への影響の仕方である。

　どんな建築を設計する時にも、その場所に固有な状況に積極的に巻き込まれて、真剣に向き合いながら解決方法を考えることが、結果的に多くの状況で共有できる価値をもつのではないかということに、私たちは今とても可能性を感じているのだと思う。その先にきっと、私たちが追い求める、愛される建築の姿があるのではないかと期待している。

get pulled into various incidents that amount to much more than just making a single building. These experiences gradually become ingrained within us, and we are able to recall them with certainty when we design. In other words, when we imagine a building, the people who we see interacting with them are neither abstract figures nor a vaguely defined impression of the people of Shodoshima in general; rather, they are real-life people, such as Yuko-chan, Kurushima-san, Tani-san, and Masako-san, and at the same time, they are new people that we have not met or have not yet been born and who will someday encounter the building. This approach, which also differs from that of making architecture through listening to specific requests and opinions of particular people, is comparable to the process in which food turns into one's blood and flesh before one knows it, and it is our slow but sure way of engaging with design.

　We currently see great potential in the idea of developing solutions for any kind of architecture that we design by actively allowing ourselves to be pulled into the situations particular to a site and engaging with the situations seriously, because we believe that doing so can in the end result in imbuing the architecture with values that can be shared in a wider variety of situations. We anticipate that this will lead us to find a piece of architecture that deserves to be cherished, which is what we are pursuing.

チャオ・ヤン

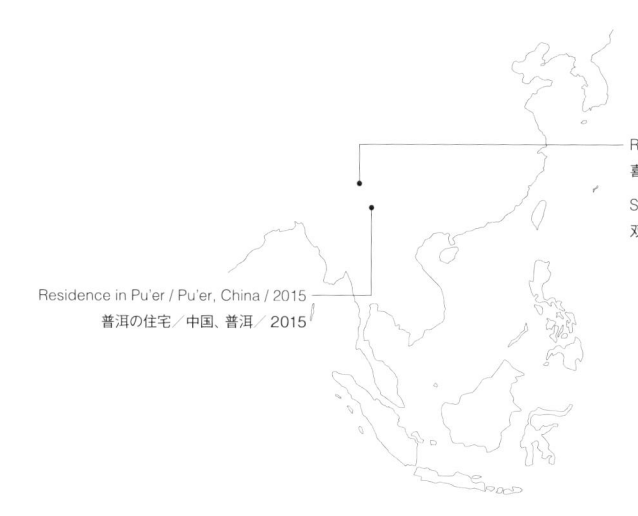

Residence in Xizhou / Dali, China / 2015
喜洲の住宅／中国、大理／ 2015

Shuangzi Hotel / Dali, China / 2015
双子ホテル／中国、大理／ 2015

Residence in Pu'er / Pu'er, China / 2015
普洱の住宅／中国、普洱／ 2015

Yang ZHAO

Introductory Essay / Erwin VIRAY

The view in Dali is breathtaking: the mountains, lake, clouds, sky. For Yang ZHAO, It is a deliberate choice to live and make his architectural operation from Dali. The place offer a convergence of interesting people of kindred spirits, seeking a quality of life, different from the cities like Beijing and Shanghai, a life that opens new possibilities in a fast changing world.

The architectural works of Yang ZHAO, look modern and abstract, a vision of now, rather than an imitation of past forms, but deep beneath there is an underlying idea that is from the past, the idea of the order in the genus loci, the order of things in a place that give it form, movement, and rhythm. Yang ZHAO strives to knowing the raison d'etre in a place, and then expressing them as they are in the new form of now. The act is courageous and visionary, in sensitively and sensibly responding to the particular conditions of approaching making architecture in a fast changing China. Though for some people there are concerns on the limitations of the seeming exoticism in the choice of Yang ZHAO, an optimistic youthfulness and company of kindred spirits expose new means of operation in an Internet connected life that is seemingly flat but in reality contoured by specificity of culture and the topography of life.

紹介文／エルウィン・ビライ

大理の眺望には息を呑む。山や湖や雲や空。チャオ・ヤンにとって、大理に住み、大理で建築活動を行うことは、熟慮の上の選択である。ここには北京や上海とは違う生活の質を求める、同族意識をもった興味深い人びとが集まっており、また素早く変わりゆく世界での新しい可能性に開けた生活がある。

チャオ・ヤンの建築作品は、モダンで抽象的な、今現在のヴィジョンに見え、過去の形態の模倣には見えないが、その根底の深い所には、過去から来るアイディア、地霊（ゲニウス・ロキ）に基づく、秩序のアイディアがある。形態、運動、リズムを生み出す、その場所の物事の秩序である。チャオ・ヤンはその場所の存在理由（レーゾン・デートル）を知ろうと努め、その上で、それらを今の新しい形態として表現する。その行為は、素早く変わりゆく中国で建築をつくろうとする特別な状況に、鋭い感受性と鋭敏な意識で応えようとする、勇気ある、予見的な行為である。チャオ・ヤンの選択に見えるうわべのエキゾチシズムの限界について懸念する向きもあるが、同族意識を伴う楽観主義的な若さの中には、インターネットと繋がった生活における、新しい方法論が垣間見える。一見単調に見えるが、現実には文化の独自性と生活の様相によって輪郭の描かれる、新しい方法論である。

大理市での冒険

スタニスラウス・ファン

雲南省大理市は中国南西部の急峻な土地で、観光のインフラには何の資本投下もされない場所であったが、1980年代に旅行ガイドブックのロンリー・プラネットが、大理を"本物の"中国として宣伝、たくさんの旅行者が押し寄せ、突然、観光開発が始まった。[1] この幸運な変化のベースになったのは自然の地形である。焦点は、洱海（アルハイ湖）とその西にある蒼山（ツァンシャン山）である。最近では中国の主要都市で大気汚染が大問題となっている中、大理市はコンスタントに旅行業の伸びを維持している。[2] その結果小さなホテルの成長が著しい。洱海の中心の金梭島（ジンシュン島）の海岸の隣接する敷地を、地元のホテル経営者が、地元の兄弟地主から、20年間の賃借期間で借りた。新しいホテルの2棟の建物は、ホテル経営者の資金で建てられ、賃借期間が終了すると地主に返還される。2012年にハーヴァード大学を卒業したチャオ・ヤンは、このプロジェクトがきっかけとなり大理に事務所を構えることになった。

Adventures in Dali

Stanislaus Fung

Dali was a sleepy place without any prior investment in tourist infrastructure in southwestern China. In the 1980s, *Lonely Planet* suddenly promoted it as an "authentic" part of China. Tens of thousands of tourists descended on the town and jumpstarted its modern development.[1] Natural topography is the basis of this change of fortune. The Erhai Lake is the focus of a series of villages and towns, with the Cangshan Mountain to its west. With air pollution a big issue in major Chinese cities in recent years, Dali has consistently maintained substantial growth in tourism.[2] Small hotels have sprung up in consequence. In the middle of the Lake, two rural landowners, brothers, leased two adjacent plots right on the coast of Jinsuo Island to a local hotelier for 20 years. A new hotel is built at the hotelier's expense which, at the end of the lease, would be handed back to the landlords as two freestanding buildings. This is the project that brought Yang ZHAO to locate his office in Dali after graduating from Harvard University in 2012.

Shuangzi Hotel
双子ホテル

Jinsuo Island, Dali, Yunnan, China 2011-2015
中国雲南省大理市金梭島（ジンシュン島）

Land for the hotel had been cleared by dynamiting a rock face on the island. The rocks obtained in this process were used in making the stone walls of the hotel, while red pine was brought by boats to make the wooden structure. Since Jinsuo Island does not have cranes, materials for walls and wooden-framed structures were handled by manual labour on site.

The design developed as two separate volumes placed at an angle to each other in order to respond to the outline of the site. Space between these volumes allows for the division of the site into two areas when the lease expires and the brothers would take over the use of the premises. To this space between the two buildings, hotel guests would be brought by boat and they would come ashore here.

Three factors are important for the mensuration of the architectural elements. First, the landowners insisted that the footprint of the buildings should be maximized to ensure that the buildings that will eventually revert to their own use would be as spacious (and valuable) as possible. Second, the carpenters of the local Bai people make wooden-framed structures of red pine, with a typical span of 3.8 m. Third, local carpenters are responsible for estimating

ホテルの敷地の、島の表土の岩石はダイナマイトで除去され、この過程で出た岩石が、ホテルの外壁に使われ、軸組の赤松は船で運ばれてきた。島にはクレーンがないので、これらの材料の組み立てはすべて人力である。

敷地の形状に合わせて、ふたつの棟が角度をつけてデザインされ、そのため賃借期間が満了した時には兄弟で分割できる。ふたつの建物の間は、ボートで運ばれた宿泊客が上陸するスペースにもなる。

建築の要素を勘案する上で、重要な3つのファクターがある。第1に、地主は、返還された時にできるだけ大きな空間を占め、価値が上がるように、建築面積を最大にすることを求めたこと。第2に、地元の白族の大工が、赤松の軸組をいつも使っている3.8mスパンで組み立てたこと。第3に、計算ではなく、彼らの経験と習慣に基づいて部材のサイズを決めたこと。これが多かれ少なかれ未だに伝統的な世界というわけで、現代の正確な計測の世界とは異なる。[3] 都市部では、中国の建築基準の規制がかかるが、地方では未だに、公式の建築認可プロセスを踏まないでも、建築することができる。

◀ Jinsuo Island from east side of Erhai lake
　アルハイ湖の東からジンシュン島を見る
▶ Shuangzi Hotel when the structure is finished
　躯体が終わった段階の双子ホテル

1: Check-in lobby
2: Lounge
3: Dinning hall
4: Cafe
5: Kitchen
6: Guestroom
7: Courtyard Suite
8: Swimming pool
9: Water yard

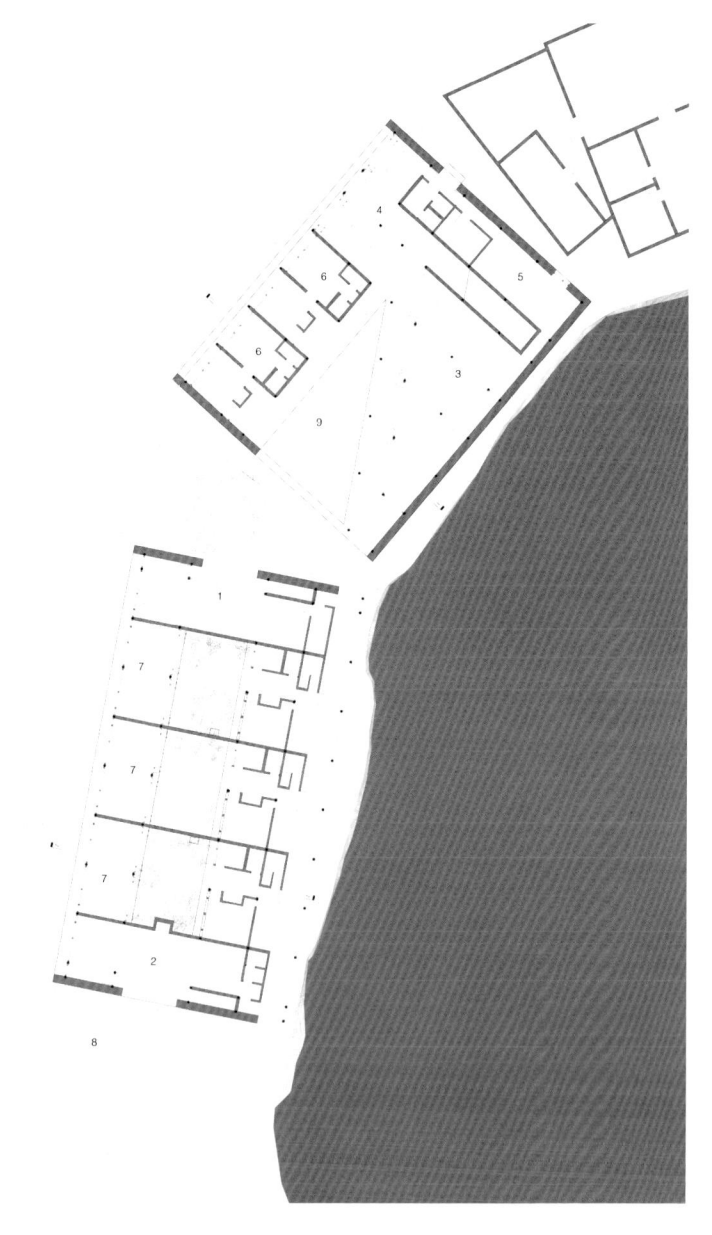

GROUND FLOOR PLAN

the sizes of wooden elements based on their experience and customs rather than by calculations. This is still a traditional world of the "more-or-less," and not the modern universe of precise measurements.[3] Chinese building codes regulate activities in urban areas, but people in rural areas can still make buildings on their land for their own use without having to deal with an official approvals process.

Local contractors are familiar with working roughly in reinforced concrete and with the methods of vernacular architecture.

1. Beth E. Notar, *Displacing Desire: Travel and Popular Culture in China* (Honolulu: University of Hawai'I Press, 2006).

2. Shanshan Dai, et al., "Distortions in Tourism Development in the Dali Autonomous Region, China," *Asia Pacific Journal of Tourism Research* 17, 2 (2012): 146-163.

3. Alexandre Koyré, *Metaphysics and Measurement: Essays in the Scientific Revolution* (Camb., MA.: Harvard University Press, 1968), 91.

▲ Rocks obtained from dynamiting the rock face next to the site.
　敷地の隣に置かれたダイナマイトで得られた岩石

▶ Stone walls are built with a local technique called "San Cha Hua"
　石の壁は"サン・チャ・フア"という地元の技法で積まれた

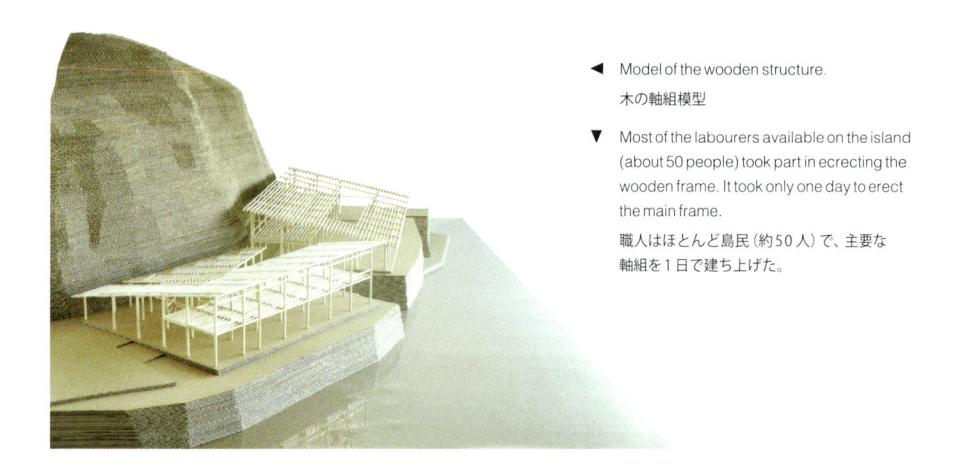

◀ Model of the wooden structure.
木の軸組模型

▼ Most of the labourers available on the island (about 50 people) took part in ecrecting the wooden frame. It took only one day to erect the main frame.
職人はほとんど島民（約50人）で、主要な軸組を1日で建ち上げた。

Stonemasons were experienced with low walls, yet the design here called for walls with a maximum height of 9 m. Tilers were experienced with traditional detailing of gable roofs but they were stumped by single-pitched roofs much larger in area than traditional roofs. Carpenters were experienced with basic framed structures but a sloped roof with a triangular cut-out created challenges for

地元の建設業者が慣れているのは、ラフな鉄筋コンクリートや地域固有の工法である。低い壁は経験がある石工に、今回は最高で9mの壁が求められた。伝統的な切妻屋根には慣れている瓦職人は、今回、面積の大きな片流れ屋根に挑戦した。基本的な軸組に慣れている大工は、今回は三角形に刳り抜かれた勾配屋根への挑戦である。こうした状況でデザインを実現するためには、チャオ・

them. These simple-sounding departures from the experience of local tradesmen meant that the architects and client had to share the role of contractor in order to execute the design. All sectional details had to be discussed using sketches and then confirmed using printouts generated by a Rhino model. In some instances, discussions on site were crucial. For instance, two kinds of tiles were used to cover vernacular buildings of the Bai people: slightly curved tiles (banwa) received

ヤンとクライアントも、施工業者の役割を分担しなければならなかった。あらゆる部分のディテールはスケッチを使って議論し、ライノセラスの3Dモデルのプリントアウトを使って確認した。時には、現場でのディスカッションは大変だった。例えば白族の人びとのヴァナキュラーな家には2種類の瓦が使われる。雨水を受けて流す、わずかに曲線をした瓦と、凸面が上を向いた円柱形の瓦である。[4] より統一感のある抽象性を目指すために、後者の瓦を使わない方針にしたため、現場で瓦職人たちと軒先のディテールを詰める必要があった。

▼ Triangular corner of the sloped roof
片流れ屋根の三角のコーナー

▲ The peripheral columns are embeded into stone walls to help resist lateral forces.
外周の柱は、水平力に抵抗するため石壁に埋め込まれた

◀ Stones from the site were shaped and placed under columns.
敷地から出た石は、削られ、柱の下にセットされた

▲ assembling the wooden frame.
木の軸組の建て込み

▼ A wooden system of columns, beams and rafters.
柱、梁、垂木の軸組

▶ Site architect discussing details with the tiler.
瓦職人と話し合う現場担当

▼ View of the roof after completion of tiling.
瓦を葺き終えた屋根を見る

rainwater channeled into them by cylindrical tiles with the convex side facing upwards (tongwa).4 The architects' proposal to omit the latter kind of tiles in order to create a more uniform and abstract effect required working out eaves details on site with the tilers.

Overall, two aspects should be noted. On the one hand, design thinking aligned programming, site organization and choice

4. Clarence Eng, *Colours and Contrast: Ceramic Traditions in Chinese Architecture* (Leiden: Brill, 2015), 38-39.

of materials with topography, orientation and situational constraints. On the other hand, in detailing and in aiming for an abstract effect, the direction of design thinking went against local conventions and habits. These two aspects oriented the direction of design development but are not aimed directly at securing specific architectural effects. Once the direction of design thinking is clarified, architectural effects emerge as an indirect result after negotiations with client and builders.

全体としてはふたつの局面が特筆される。ひとつは、プログラム、現場の組織、材料の選択、そして地形、方位、束縛条件に添ってデザインが進められたこと。もうひとつは、ディテールを考え、抽象性を狙った時に、ローカルの慣習や工法と、デザインの方向性が対立したことである。このふたつの局面はデザインの方向を向いてはいたが、特別な建築的な成果を獲得することを直接目指したわけではなかった。一度デザインの方向性が明らかになれば、建築的な成果は、クライアント、建設業者との交渉の末に、間接的に結実する。

▼ View of the trianglar courtyard from the south after completion of the structural frame.
躯体完成後の三角形のコートヤードを南から見る

◀ View of the trianglar courtyard from the north after completion of the structural frame.
躯体完成後の三角形のコートヤードを北から見る

COPPER SHEET 0.3

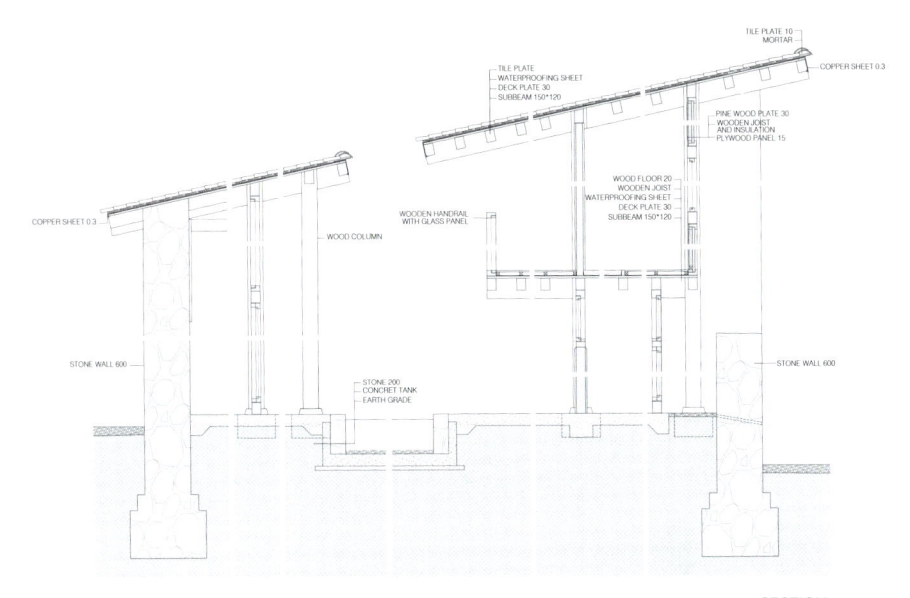

TILE PLATE
WATERPROOFING SHEET
DECK PLATE 30
SUBBEAM 150*120

TILE PLATE 10
MORTAR

COPPER SHEET 0.3

PINE WOOD PLATE 30
WOODEN JOIST
AND INSULATION
PLYWOOD PANEL 15

WOOD COLUMN

WOODEN HANDRAIL
WITH GLASS PANEL

WOOD FLOOR 20
WOODEN JOIST
WATERPROOFING SHEET
DECK PLATE 30
SUBBEAM 150*120

STONE WALL 600

STONE 200
CONCRETE TANK
EARTH GRADE

STONE WALL 600

SECTION

Residence in Xizhou
喜洲の住宅

Xizhou, Dali, Yunnan, China 2014-2015
中国雲南省大里市喜洲

▲ Sketch by the client giving an impression of the future house.
　クライアントから渡された、未来の家のスケッチ

▼ Birdview of the building with its surroundings.
　住宅と周辺の鳥瞰

On the western shore of Erhai Lake, Yang ZHAO designed a house in the village of Xizhou for a painter and his wife. The site is located on the eastern edge of the village, next to green fields. Traditional courtyard houses in the village typically have east-facing main buildings flanked by smaller buildings on both sides. The new house responds to the demands of local residents for good geomancy: the related level of the ground floor is set at a uniform level that is in keeping with the ground floors of neighboring buildings. In common with the inward-looking character of courtyard houses in the village, the new house also has an introvert character. The use of lime plaster mixed with straw—a very common form of rendering for external walls in Xizhou—also helps relate the new house to its context.

チャオ・ヤンは、アルハイ湖の西岸、喜洲に、画家夫妻のために住宅を設計した。敷地は村落の東端に位置し、緑野に面している。村落の典型的なコートヤード住宅の主屋は東向きで両側に小さな棟を従えている。この新しい家は住人のジオマンシー（土占い）の要求に従って、1階床レベルを隣接する建物と同じレベルに設定した。周囲のコートヤード・ハウスの内側を向いた特性と同様に、この家も内向きの性格をもっている。喜洲の外壁材として一般的な、藁を混ぜた漆喰を使ったことも、周囲のコンテクストに溶け込ませる結果を生んだ。

SITE PLAN

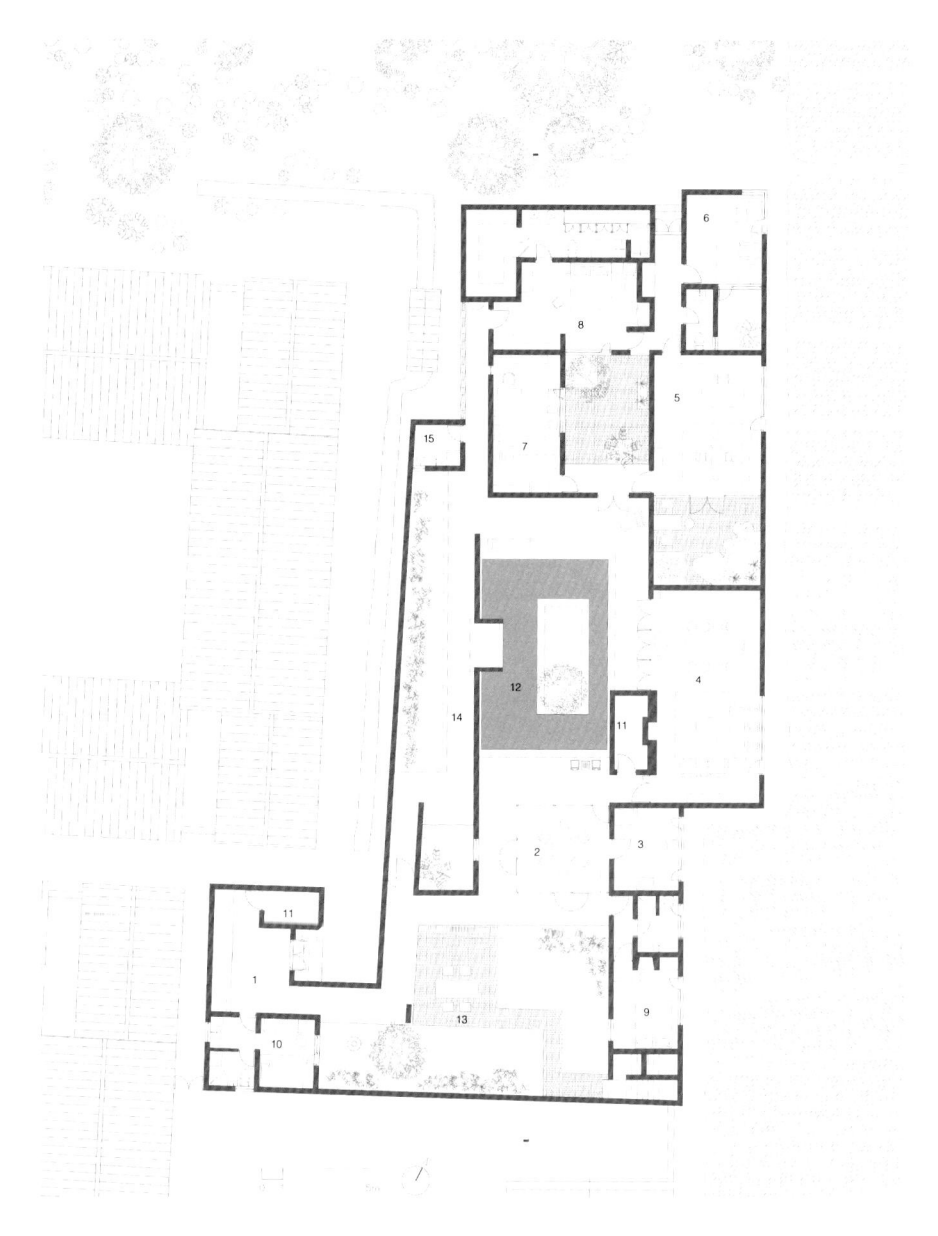

1: Entry
2: Dining room
3: Kitchen
4: Living room
5: Artist's studio
6: Artist's study
7: Wife's study
8: Master bedroom
9: Guestroom
10: Maid room
11: Storage
12: Water yard
13: Front yard
14: Bamboo Passage
15: Laundry

GROUND FLOOR PLAN

Inside, the house is divided into the private quarters of the resident couple to the north, and a series of living areas and accommodation for a guest and a live-in cleaner/cook to the south. Nine courtyards of varying sizes show the designer's concern to reduce the scale of the traditional courtyard house and to match courtyards with various rooms. The circulation through the main parts of the house develops as an alternation between spatial compression and spatial dilation. The entry sequence in the southwest involves two 180-degree turns that bring the visitor to the southern courtyard. A long corridor offers quick access to the private quarters, with a glimpse of the central shallow pond halfway. From the southern courtyard one can walk undercover past an enclosed dining area towards the pond. Yang Z HAO has deleted the conventional verandahs along the sides of courtyards. A storage room plays a quiet role in this and also obscures the size of the main living

内部は夫婦の私的領域を北に配し、リビング関連の諸室とゲストルーム、住み込みの掃除人、コックの部屋を南側に配した。いろいろなサイズの9つのコートヤードを設けたのは、伝統的なコートハウスのスケールを縮小し、各部屋に合わせたコートヤードをつくったからで、主要部分を循環すると、縮小した空間と膨張した空間が交互に展開していく。南西のエントランス部分のシークエンスを見ると、180度ターンを2回させて、訪問者を南のコートヤードに向かわせる。途中で中央の細い池がチラッと見える長い廊下を使えば、プライベートな領域に早くアクセスできる。南のコートヤードからは閉じたダイニングエリアの横をこっそり池の方に歩いていくこともできる。昔からコートヤードの横にはベランダがつくられるのだが、チャオ・ヤンはあえてつくらなかった。この点で、収納が静かにその役割を果たし、またメインリビングのサイズを分かりにくくしているが、東の緑野や中心の池や、西側のパッセージに植えられた竹の向こうには、ツァンシャン山が見える。プライベートの領域には、大きさ

▼ View towards the water yard from the south
水の庭を南から見る

▲ View towards the water yard from the living room.
水の庭を居間から見る

◀ View towards the water yard from the north.
水の庭を北から見る

▼ View of the front yard
前庭を見る

area, with views out to the eastern green fields as well as to the central pond and, above the bamboos of the western passage, to Cangshan Mountain to the west. The private quarters are organized around four courtyards of different sizes and orientation. This variety continues the attempt to introduce daylight from the east and the west in the living room, so that the atmosphere of various spaces will be appreciably different at different times of the day.

と方位の違う4つのコートヤードがある。この多様性はリビングにも続き、東、そして西からの日射しを採り入れ、時間ごとに異なった雰囲気を各部屋にもたらす。

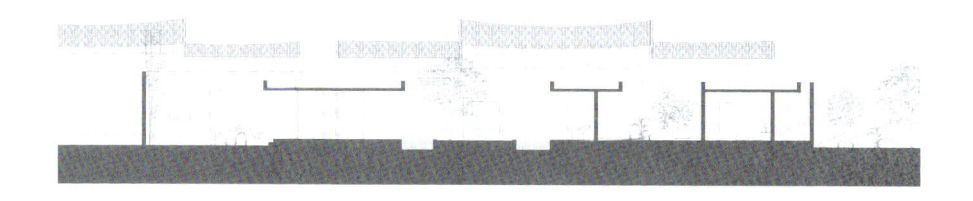

SECTION

Structural elements of the house are kept out of view by setting the thickness of walls to 200 mm so that columns and in-fill walls are indistinguishable once they are rendered. The maximum span of 8 m on one side of the southern courtyard required a beam that is 600 mm deep. However, this and other beams of various dimensions are kept unobtrusive by placing them above rather than below roof slabs. By subordinating structural expression, light and spatial effects, and the client's collection of furniture are allowed to draw one's attention. Simplification of detailing has allowed the designer to respond to budgetary considerations: for example, stone capping on the top of walls was omitted to reduce cost. The tops of walls slope away from wall surfaces so that rainwater would not run onto them and stain them.

柱などの構造要素は、200mmの壁厚の中に隠されて表面からは見えない。南のコートヤードの最大8mのスパンには、600mm成の梁が架けられているが、これを含め、さまざまなサイズの梁は、邪魔にならないように屋根スラブの上に出っ張る逆梁としている。構造要素を副次的に扱うことによって、光と空間の効果や、クライアントの家具コレクションの方に目が行くようにしている。予算への配慮からディテールはシンプルにされ、例えば壁の上端の石の笠木はコストを減らすために省略されている。壁の上端は雨水が壁を汚さないよう、壁の表面側から離れる方に傾斜している。コートヤードにより内部と外部の関係が繰り返され、異なる時刻、異なる場所で、さまざまな印象を与えることを優先するために、仕上げや構成部材の物質性をフェティッシュに操作することはしない。[5]

▲ View of the house from agricultural field.
緑野から住宅を見る

◄ View of bamboo corridor.
竹の廊下を見る

In giving primacy to the iteration of inside-outside relationships in a series of courtyards, and to the varying impressions of an environment from different vantage points at various times, the design thinking here rejects the fetishistic manipulation of the materiality of surfaces and of object-components.[5] "Courtyard house" is not about the stability and repeatability of a type but the pretext of a series of individuations that echo each other.

"コートヤード・ハウス"とここでいうのは繰り返される安定した住居タイプのことを指しているのではなく、お互いに呼応する個別なコートの一群を指している。

5. Cf. Dong Yugan, "Sui xingzhi qi: BeijingHongzhuanMeishu guanshiji," in *Wu You Yuan*, Volume 1: Huihuayuyuanlin, ed. JinQiuye& Wang Xin (Shanghai: TongjiDaxuechubanshe, 2015), 88-109; Zhou Yi, "HongzhuanMeishuguansanshi," in *Wu You Yuan*, 110-119.

Residence in Pu'er
普洱の住宅

Pu'er, Yunnan, China 2014-2015
中国雲南省普洱市

▲ View of the house from the hill
　丘の上から住宅を見る

▶ View of the house from the street
　通りから住宅を見る

Yang Zhao's international reputation has gradually spread to other cities in southwestern China in the last two years. In Pu'er, a city about 300 km from his base in Dali, a client had asked for a house in which three generations of his family would live together. The site is in an affluent area with freestanding villas, mostly three storeys high. The new house is a three-storey structure of grey off-form concrete walls textured with rough wooden formwork. This direct expression of concrete and a refusal to express a preference for a colour marks a humble but uncompromising posture against the light pink and yellow buildings nearby. A curved boundary wall on the north side acts as a buffer against traffic noise. Major spaces of the house are oriented to the hill on the southwestern side of the site since this orientation is relatively private.

On the ground floor, the west and south

チャオ・ヤンの国際的名声は中国南西部の他の都市でも、過去2年間で次第に広まった。大理市から300km離れた普洱（プーアル）で、3世代の家族が一緒に住むための住宅を依頼された。敷地は、主に3階建ての富裕層のヴィラが建っている地域にある。新しい家は、ラフな木製型枠の打ち放しのグレー色の3階建ての住宅である。コンクリートの直截な表現、そして色彩の拒否は、近辺の派手なピンクやイエローの建物に対して、慎ましいが妥協しない姿勢を示している。

北側の敷地境界の壁の曲面は道路の騒音の緩衝帯になっている。家の主要室は、南西側の比較的プライベートな、丘の側を向いている。

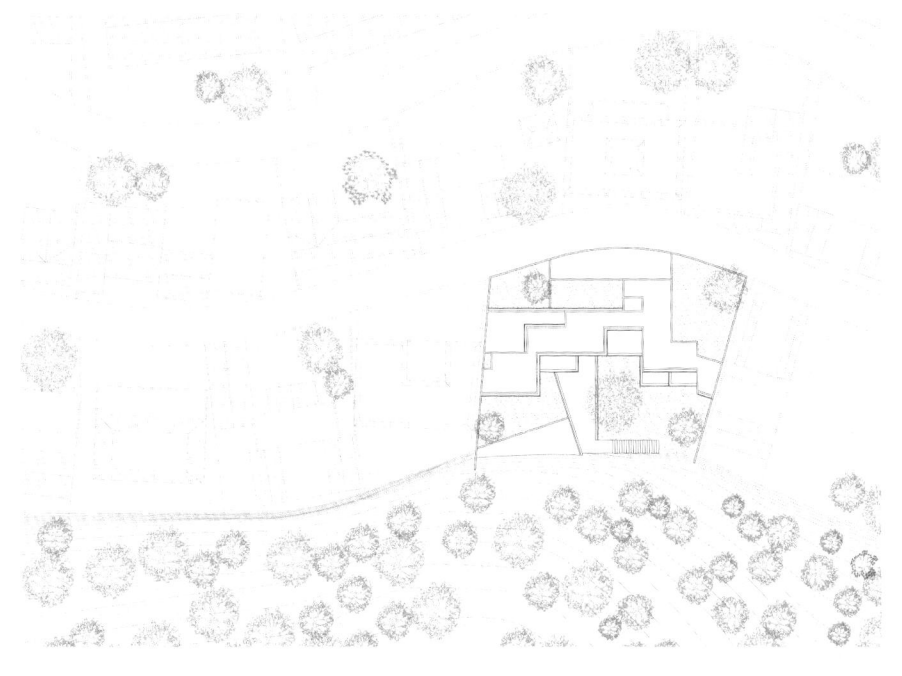

SITE PLAN 1:1000

▲ Model photo from the south
南から見た模型

▶ Model photo from the north
北から見た模型

1: Hallway
2: Living area
3: Dining area
4: Tea room
5: Kitchen
6: Laundry
7: Sauna
8: Movie room
9: Storage
10: Maid's room
11: Grandparents' room
12: East entrance yard
13: Pool
14: North entrance yard
15: South garden
16: West garden

gardens seem to engage interior spaces in a game of "pushing hands," the Chinese exercise aimed at promoting focus and a sense of balance. Structure is highly irregular with walls placed on the northern part of the plan and steel columns along the edge of the north and south courts. The rough texture of walls, kept the same indoors as well as outdoors, contribute an atmospheric but backgrounded quality. Internal walls have been minimized so that furniture marks the foci of a meandering field. The number of columns has been minimized also and those that remain are painted black to make them inconspicuous. The maximum span of 7.5 m in one location, unusual for a three-story building, required an upturned beam 400 mm deep. The contours of the hill provided two clues for

1階の西と南の庭に削られたインテリア空間は"推手"(集中力を高め、バランス感覚を鍛える中国のエクササイズ)のゲームをやっているように見える。構造は、壁が北側に集まり、鉄骨の柱が南北のコートの端部に配置された、非常にイレギュラーな形をしている。内部の壁も外と同じようにラフなテクスチャーなので、趣きのある、裏面のような感じを醸している。内部の間仕切り壁は最小限にされているので、椅子やテーブルが曲がりくねった平面の焦点になる。柱も最小限に小さくされて、目立たないように黒く塗られ

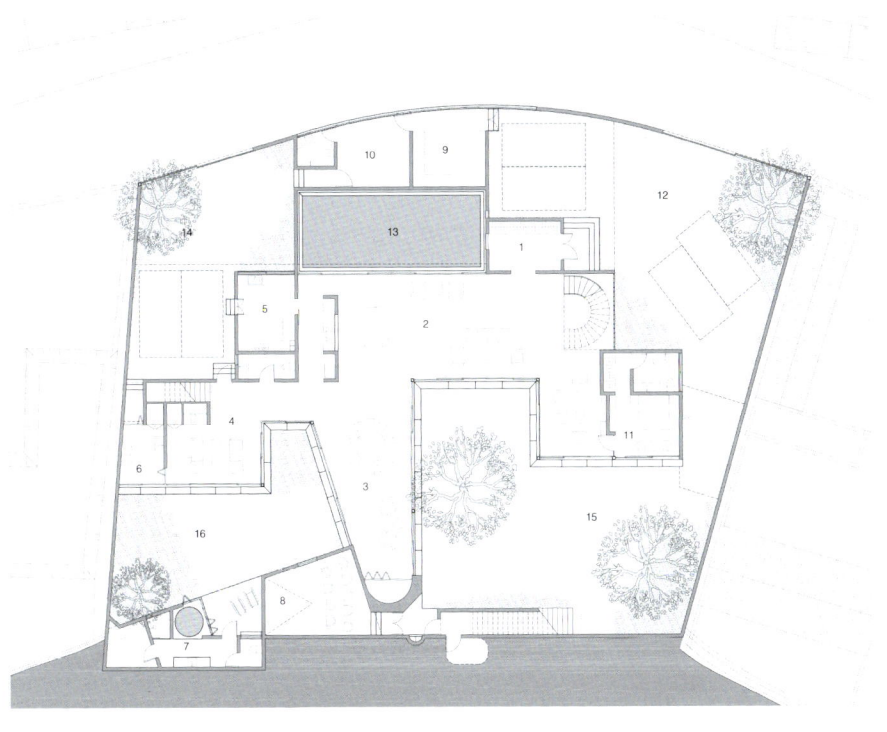

GROUND FLOOR PLAN

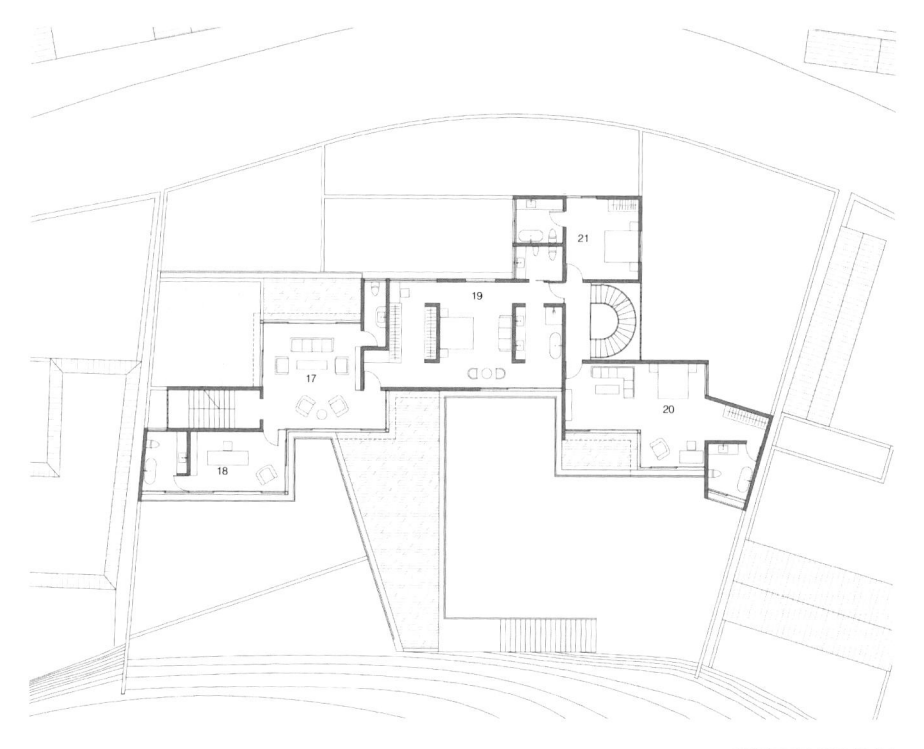

SECOND FLOOR PLAN

17: Family room
18: Study room
19: Master bedroom
20: Elder daughter's room
21: Maid's room
22: Meditation room
23: Younger daughter's room
24: Guest room

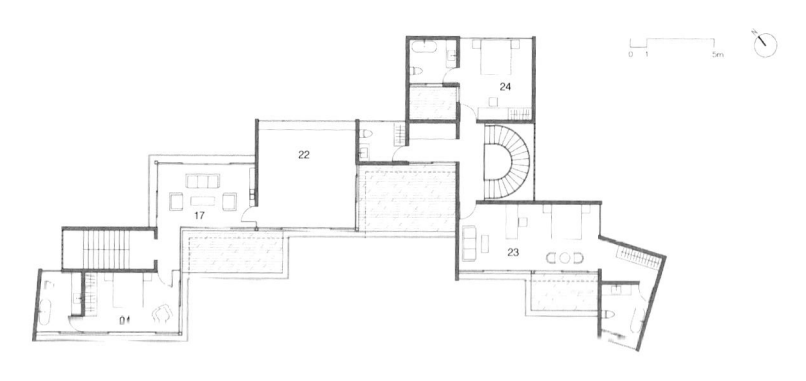

THIRD FLOOR PLAN

▲ View towards west garden through the dinning
ダイニングから北庭方向を見る

the ground floor plan. The edge of the sauna and movie room facing the west garden is a continuation of the hillscape that introduces a diagonal geometry to the plan. The contours of the hills facing the south garden allows a staircase to follow the orthogonal geometry of the house. The geometry of the dining area is a consequence of topography (see page 179, GROUND FLOOR PLAN).

While the plan of the ground floor plays out its game of inside/outside, balconies and full-height glazing on the second and third floors create a theatre-like relation to life in the southern courtyards below. On the second floor, corridors have been minimized by creating a suite of rooms. But privacy issues of the bedrooms meant that the location of walls (and structural considerations) are

ている。3階建てにはあまりやらない最大スパン7.5mの部分の梁は、400mm成の逆梁になった。丘のコンターが1階平面にふたつの糸口を与えた。西の庭に面するサウナ室とムービー室のエッジは丘の地形から続いていて、平面に対角線のジオメトリーをもち込んでいる。南の庭の階段についてはこの家の直角のジオメトリーに従っている。ダイニングエリアの形はトポグラフィの結果である。(179ページ GROUND FLOOR PLAN参照)1階平面では内部／外部のゲームがやりつくされたが、2階、2階のバルコニーと天井いっぱいにされた開口が、下の南のコートヤードに劇場のような関係性をつくった。2階は部屋をひとつながりにすることによって廊下を最小限にした。しかし寝室のプライバシーの問題から壁の配置（と構造の考え方）が1階とは異なっている。

181

▲ View of living room
▼ リビングを見る

quite different to the ground floor situation. A process of "pushing hands" had to be extended from the ground floor to modulate the spatial delineation of the upper floors. In order to maintain a sense of openness towards the south for the major rooms upstairs, circulation issues had to be minimized by generating suites rooms.

The difficulty of the design lies in the question of how consistency of approach and conception can be maintained. As Yang ZHAO actively responded to realistic issues one by one, design decisions can easily become piecemeal. Since it is beyond the scope of this presentation to study the models and drawings of the design process in detail, we can only offer a glimpse of what is entailed by "pushing hands." Issues of orientation and privacy and the intention to create an open relationship between major internal spaces and the west and south gardens are the major factors sustaining a sense of tension in the design process. This sense of tension informs the hybrid structural system, with walls on one side and steel columns with a maximum span of 7.5 m, along the other side. The use of upturned beams to create a clear ceiling plane avoids the possibility of beams under floor slabs to detract from the openness of inside and outside. "Pushing hands" is a process that

"推手"のプロセスは上階にも適用され、空間の輪郭が調整された。南へ開かれた感じを維持するため、部屋を連続させて、サーキュレーションの問題は最小に限定された。いかに計画へのアプローチと考え方の一貫性を維持できるかに、デザインの難しさがあった。チャオ・ヤンが現実的な問題にひとつひとつ精力的に対処するに従って、ひとつひとつの決定行為が容易になっていった。デザイン・プロセスの模型やドローイングを詳細に提示することは、このプレゼンテーションの範囲を超えてしまうため、"推手"によって何が起きたかは、ほんの少ししか示すことができない。方位とプライバシーの問題、そして主要な内部空間と西と南の庭をオープンに関係付けようとする意図は、デザイン・プロセスの中で緊張感を維持する重要なファクターである。片側は壁で、もう一方の側は大スパン7.5mの鉄骨の柱で構成されるという、ハイブリッドな構造システムは、この緊張感がもたらしたものである。

スラブの下に梁が出っ張るという、内部、外部の開放性を壊す事態を避けるため、逆梁によってすっきりした天井面を実現させた。

"推手"は、方位からオープン・プランへ、構造や施工の問題へ段階的に推移する、緊張関係にあるさまざまなファクターに声や媒体を与えるひとつのプロセスである。段階的な推移の間、デザインの選択肢を逐一選別することによって、目標の一貫性は明確にされ、維持された。

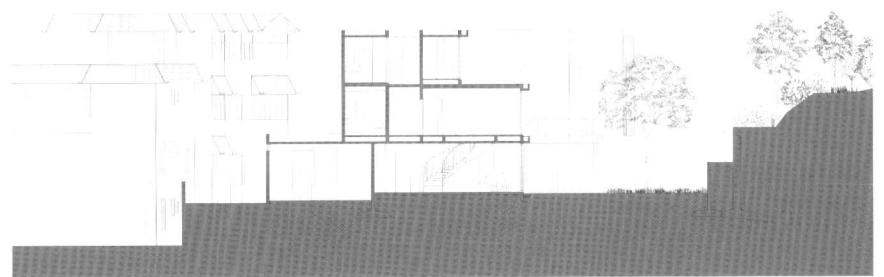

SECTION

gives voice and agency to various factors in tension and involves a set of devolutions from orientation to open plan, to structural and constructional issues. By sorting through permutations of design possibilities while engaging a series of devolutions, a consistency of purpose is clarified and sustained.

In the projects presented above, Yang ZHAO emerges as someone looking for unexpected ways of building that lurks in the midst of known factors, forces and techniques. This involves unsettling the builders' habits and a refusal of traditional meanings of vernacular patterns and symbols. In this sense, we may consider the projects presented here under the sign of *déjà vu*. The buildings on Jinsuo Island and in Xizhou evoke a generalized memory of the Chinese vernacular. The house in Pu'er seem to harken to a generalized memory of modernism. And yet there is a persistent sense of difference. The projects suspended certain forms of procedural memory (habits and ways of building) and semantic memory (vernacular styling, ornaments, symbols) and appear to stir up a kind of allomnesia, attributing to past experiencea new content or context. In each instance, even though the designer had been engaging a present potential, this "being-possible" might be "retrospectively experienced as always-having-been possible."[6] This can be sharply distinguished from a traditionalist or regionalist approach that would reify the past or the local into a "content" for continual re-application in different contexts.

これまで紹介してきたプロジェクトの中で、チャオ・ヤンは、既知のファクターや能力、テクニックの中に隠れている、予期しない建築の方法を探求する人として現れている。これには、施工者の慣習を揺るがせることや、ヴァナキュラーなパターンやシンボルの昔からの意味を拒否することが含まれる。この意味では、ここに示したプロジェクトは、デジャヴの兆候の下にあると考えられるかもしれない。ジンシュン島(きしゅう)や貴州の建物は、中国のヴァナキュラーの普遍化した記憶を呼び覚まし、普洱(プーアル)の住宅はモダニズムの普遍化した記憶を呼び覚ますかも知れない。しかしそこには一貫して差異の感覚がある。

これらのプロジェクトは手続き的記憶(慣習や工法)と意味論的記憶(ヴァナキュラーな様式、装飾、シンボル)のある種の形態を吊り下げており、新しい意味や内容が過去の経験に起源があるとする、一種の記憶錯誤を呼び起こしているようにみえる。どちらの場合も、チャオ・ヤンは今現在の可能性を探求しているとしても、この"今可能なこと"は"過去に経験したいつもそうだった可能性"[6]かもしれない。このことは、過去や地方をコンテンツとして、異なるコンテクストの中で繰り返し再利用する、伝統主義者や地方主義者のアプローチとは画然と区別されるだろう。

6. Paolo Virno, *Déjà Vu and the End of History*, trans. David Broder (London: Verso, 2015), 16.

(Stanislaus Fung is Associate Professor and Director of the MPhil-PhD programme in the School of Architecture, Chinese University of Hong Kong.)

(馮仕達 Stanislaus Fungは香港中文大学の建築学部、修士・博士課程の准教授およびディレクター)

▲ View of the house from the hill
丘から住宅を見る

Far Afield from the Ocean Current

Teppei FUJIWARA

Why Asia?

To be honest, when I first heard about the idea of making GALLERY·MA's 30th anniversary exhibition a group show on five young Asian architects, I wondered why the show's focus had to be limited on Asia as a region. The 25th anniversary exhibition held five years ago was themed on "Global Ends", and it reported on how individualistic architecture that could not be fully explained by only their regional contexts were emerging in a world taken over by globalism. Was it necessary to focus on Asia again just five years after individuals were shown to be creatively responding to the world and to history at large with their unique individuality while transcending the framework of the geographic region? When I asked Mr. Viray and GALLERY·MA's planning team about this, they told me that they had their minds on the Great East Japan Earthquake. They wanted to make an exhibition that would give courage and hope to the young architects and students who had lost spirit in the wake of the great tragedy. The once-in-a-hundred-year disaster came at a time when Japan had already been suffering from what would come to be called the "Japan Syndrome"—a predicament in which a multitude of high-order societal risks, such as population aging, rapid population shrinkage, economic stagnation, income decline, employment uncertainty, social insecurity, and community breakdown, all occur at once. Four years have gone by since then, but Japanese society is still tense. While hope is not something that should be spoken of lightly, I can most certainly understand why one would feel that this is precisely why hope is what is needed.

But what sort of hope can we convey by working with the subject of Asia? If the intent is to instill hope from a viewpoint that says "Because Asia is in the midst of rapid economic growth", I for one would not feel any hope in such an idea. A good economy is not what gets architecture built; if anything, an overly powerful market will only simplify the formation of architecture.

We live in a difficult age today. Great social crises such as large-scale disasters and financial crises—tremendous events in the face of which we are powerless as individuals—are occurring frequently around the world right beside our everyday lives. What I personally want this exhibition to present are human responses to this situation and a sense of what direction the architecture that is being born from Asian philosophies, religions, and cultural climates in this difficult age—architecture that has a place in civilizational discourse—is heading in. What could be an architecture that will bring with it a hope with which we will be able to overcome this difficult age?

Singapore / LING Hao
Spaces for Animate Beings Woven into an Artificial City

When I got out at the airport, I was taken aback by how hot it was even though it was February. I should have expected as much: the world map in the plane had shown me that I was practically right on the Equator. It was 50 years ago that Lee Kuan Yew shed tears of anguish as he declared an undesired independence. The success that Singapore, a nation composed of some 60 small islands, has since achieved is the fruit of his experimental urban and economic policies that have deservedly been described as radical.

We had booked a hotel for our stay in Singapore in a quaint neighborhood known as Little India. Little India was lined with shophouses that formed exciting passages known as five-foot ways in Malaysia and qilou arcades in Taiwan. I was surprised to find this great piece of urban tissue because I had been picturing the cityscape to be crowded with skyscrapers based on my arbitrary preconceptions.

With his distinctive look and relaxed air, LING Hao showed up at our hotel in the manner of a kung-fu master who had casually dropped in on a neighbor. Although a Malaysian national, he had studied architecture in Singapore and Sydney and was now working in Singapore. We soon found out that he worked very freely: He did not employ any staff or own an office space, and he did his design work on a MacBook Pro that he carried with him while wandering around like a nomad. We were aware that he designed some large projects, so we asked him how he managed to handle them. He explained that he collaborated with an architect couple—friends from college—whenever his projects were relatively large. After he had given us a presentation of his projects in the hotel's café, he handed us a small, self-published portfolio that consisted mostly of very tasteful monochromatic CAD drawings. The work captured his highly refined aesthetic sense and his relaxed, easy-going deportment.

The building by LING Hao that we saw the next day was just as striking as the architect's appearance. What left the strongest impression on me was the wind that flowed through the building. I could feel a gentle breeze in every part of it. Meanwhile, the spaces were boldly scaled. Much larger than the scale of the human body, the generous spaces that I was enveloped in had more of a landscape scale.

LING Hao holds a great affection for the city—just as one might expect of someone who recommended to us the quaint neighborhood of Little India. When explaining his projects, he will always start by giving a commentary on the formation of a site's urban tissue. His spaces may be full of fresh sensibilities, but his architectural ideas are serious. Singapore is a manmade city-state where even the jungles are grown artificially. Even while fully understanding this artificiality, LING Hao interprets the artificial environment organically and attempts to respond to it with architecture of a biological nature. I am greatly moved by the presence of the animate, life-filled spaces that he has woven into the tissues of the city.

Dali / Yang ZHAO
Resonance between Architecture that Stands Apart

We flew out from Singapore to Shanghai on a late night flight and connected directly to a domestic Chinese airline to Dali. I could really appreciate the vastness of the Earth after having traveled all the way at once from the equatorial island group to the mountain range that extended to Tibet. The season also changed back to winter from summer. Dali, a famous source of marble, was a city that had long prospered through trade with Myanmar and Tibet.

 We all had assumed that Yang ZHAO was from Dali, but he explained that he had moved to the city after he had taken a liking to it during his travels (he was actually from Chongqing). Set before a lake with the magnificent Cangshan mountain range behind it, the location certainly looked like it could be a theatre set for a mythical tale, and the old streets built in marble were beautiful. Even so, the ease with which he made such a decision was quite incredible. After I did some research, I learned that Dali was known to be a place where backpackers found themselves staying for extended periods of time, and it was home to many people who moved there from both in and outside the country. This apparently had to do with the fact that many of the Bai people, an ethnic minority, lived in the Dali region. The story seemed to be that the central government had kept its political intervention to a gentle level out of regard for the minority group, and this had enabled the multi-language/multicultural society of the old Eurasian trade city to survive.

 Yang laughingly told us that he was most probably the first "architect" in Dali's history. The reason why he made a home for himself and his family and set up an office in Dali—a land so remote that he had to explain to his clients what a design fee was— apparently was not only because the city was beautiful and a junction of various cultures but also because it possessed a culture of carpentry and crafts. The very circumstances in which he was able to make architecture through taking time to talk with craftsmen was a rarity in China; moreover, it seemed like he had moved away from the realms of the megacities such as Beijing and Shanghai in order to keep a distance from demands for economic speed and excessive efficiency. What he had assumed was a creative attitude of purposely "standing apart".

Incidentally, many of Yang's buildings literally stand apart in isolation. They have simple, bold forms with beautiful proportions appropriate for architecture that stand alone in the midst of grandiose natural landscapes. It is not just an issue of proportion and form though; the chemistry between the solids and voids and the solids and frames that speak to each other are what make his buildings resonate powerfully with their surroundings.

We rode a boat out to a small island on the lake to see Yang ZHAO's projects that were still under construction. The two projects on the island were both hotels; they needed to be accessed by boat because of the island's difficult roads. The projects spoke strongly of a conscious effort to make the approach paths to the buildings a part of the architectural experience and of an interest to shape the spaces in a garden-like way as a response to their isolated character. The idea of the garden seemed to be an important spatial concept that spanned both Japan and China; this was something that I had also felt strongly from the work of the Hangzhou architect WANG Shu.

When we were walking along a path in a fishing village, Yang ZHAO abruptly pointed at the perimeter wall of a house that rose up at a street corner and introduced the wall to us as his teacher of architecture. The wall had a distinctive elevation like that of a mille-feuille pastry and comprised a total of about 10 layers: four bottom layers of stacked stone of different textures, three mud layers, two layers finished in plaster, and a timber frame structure with a tiled roof at the top. Yang ZHAO told us that the local carpenters had taught him the significance of each layer. The wall, which could not be explained simply in terms of functionality, had an awesomeness to it that made it seem like it was an architectural manifestation of the spirit of human history. Were these the kind of wondrous things that the attitude of "standing apart" enabled one to encounter?

Ho Chi Minh City / VO Trong Nghia
In Front of Where Architecture Faces

The series of bamboo buildings that Nghia has been experimenting with since early in his career is unmistakably what makes up the core of his architectural work. His work in bamboo is not only interesting for its unique construction methods, details, and forms; there is also much to be said about Nghia's great skill as a producer who has even organized a team of craftsmen specialized in the construction of bamboo architecture. Nghia studied architecture in Japan under Hiroshi Naito, but his work also shows the influence of the project for a university in Ho Chi Minh City that he co-designed with Kazuhiro Kojima. He also seems to have a way of projecting strong messages like Tadao Ando. If you take into account the avid interest and intellectual curiosity that he has shown toward Japanese architects as role models and his extraordinary ability to take action, it is understandable why he has become the success story that he is today with two offices in Ho Chi Minh City and Hanoi and several dozen staff members.

Out of all of his many talents and achievements, what I would like to focus on is his House for Trees projects. Nghia has taken a highly critical stand on the practice of architects designing custom-made houses. This may be painful to the ears of young architects in Japan, where it is common for architects to start out by designing houses. Even though Nghia may have learned a lot from Japan, he also views Japan with a sharply critical eye.

The fundamental question that he asks is: What will we do about unchecked urban sprawl and our cities that have been filled up with artificial constructions? He has chosen to respond to this with an idea to not make houses to merely be houses and to instead look at houses as opportunities for bringing nature back to the city. The House for Trees—what does the architecture face toward (i.e. what is it for?)? There is something powerful about this stance through which Nghia is addressing the essence of the issue in such a simple manner. If Nghia continues to build with the concept of the House for Trees, forests may soon really begin to emerge within the cities of Vietnam.

During my stay in Ho Chi Minh City, I was told again and again, "Fujiwara-san, you should meditate too." Nghia actually held morning and afternoon meditation sessions at his offices. He apparently incorporated the same method of meditation through which the Buddha had found Enlightenment. Nghia explained to me that, being as busy as he was with so many projects, he was able to become more creative by shutting out the outside world and focusing his spirit through meditation. It again stung to hear him say that the tradition of meditation was the most important thing being lost from Japanese culture. There is no question that Nghia is the person who should be introduced as Vietnam's forerunning architect. Even though Nghia may already run a large firm with many staff members, and even though his many achievements may be blurring his ideas, I feel great hope for the architecture of our difficult age in the radical attitude through which Nghia is questioning what lies beyond where architecture is headed by asking what it is for.

Tokyo / Maki ONISHI+Yuki HYAKUDA
Human Living and Architecture

The office of Maki ONISHI and Yuki HYAKUDA is located at a street corner in a low-lying neighborhood of Tokyo. Gaping wide open to the street in the manner of a print shop or tofu store, the office space has no window fixtures and is completely exposed to the wind (they do have a vinyl curtain that they use in the winter). I have the impression that their architectural work has been gradually changing ever since they relocated to this office. Having been active since when they were university students, the architect duo has always been free and unconstrained by conventional thinking. Rather than becoming more "grown-up" through gaining experience, however, if anything they are becoming more serious about being unconstrained by convention. At times they will even work on things that do not seem like architecture.

By observing them to see what their main theme is, I have noticed that they seem to be interested in not only architecture but in human living as a whole. This approach of thinking about things from human living is nothing unique to them; it is a trend that can be seen widely among young architects and students in Japan (if viewed from outside Japan, they may perhaps be thought of as the "children" of Atelier Bow-Wow). However, even though there is an appeal to the idea of thinking about the relationships between architecture and human living, in reality it is not such an easy issue. After all, the notion of living is amorphous and difficult to get a handle on. In o+h's case, they do not even employ Atelier Bow-Wow's approach of analyzing architectural typologies; in fact, they seem to be trying to avoid this by working with what seems like a ludic, experimental approach. For instance, at one time they tried enclosing the realm of human living inside a building designed like an oddly shaped container; at another time they made a scattering of defined places for the activities of human living to form around; and at another time they even conceived a strange device meant to generate certain activities of human living. They also seem to have an interest in other mediums, such as books, exhibitions, and plays. Perhaps this is only to be expected because books, exhibitions, and plays also deal with capturing the amorphous concept of human living and giving it forms and names.

But what do they see in the direction that they are heading? To me, it seems that what they are trying to do is to create what could be called "endless stories". Stories, for better or worse, will always have closure. On the other hand, there is no way of marking the beginning or end of an architectural experience. I am under the impression that that they are trying to create endless stories by working with a genre of architecture that offers an "endless experience"—and this is why they are avoiding ideas of typology that will tie down their stories to set forms of architecture more than they want. This may perhaps be a unique attitude of architecturalizing the non-architectural. I am personally very interested in seeing what lies ahead of the exploration with architectural alchemy aimed at generating endless stories and formless, amoeba or slime mold-like architecture that is being spearheaded by o+h in the world of contemporary Japanese architecture.

Bangkok / Chat CHUENRUDEEMOL
"Thaibrids" in the City of Animate Beings

Unusually for this day and age, Chat does not have a website for his office. This made it a challenge to obtain any information about him. The first things that I found were his personal residence and research on vernacular shacks in Bangkok that he had uploaded to Facebook. The research on the shacks included some powerful spaces that almost led me to believe that they were designed by Chat. The forceful photographs from his research were enough to make me develop a confidence in his talent.

My friend who is knowledgeable about Thailand would often affectionately say, "Thailand is a country that will assimilate anything." When I actually visited Bangkok, what I saw was indeed a mix of various cultures: American-style shopping malls, Japanese-style department stores and convenient stores, etc.

"Thai-ness? There is no such thing as Thai-ness. Thai-ness is how everything is assimilated and hybridized." The ever-cheerful Chat had been telling me this when he invented the word "Thaibrid". At one moment he had been talking passionately about how uniquely wonderful the bamboo crafts made in the different Thai farming villages that his wife had been researching were, but then he asserted that there was no such thing as Thai-ness in the next. And then he went on to show me posters to tell me how much he loved Jacques Tati's films.

We later got around to understanding that the shacks that we were so strongly drawn to were shelters built to house the workers on Bangkok's large construction sites. They formed temporary informal "villages" in the city. The construction workers in Bangkok were mostly migrant laborers from outside the city and the country, and the settlements that they made on large construction sites could become like housing developments. Markets selling daily goods and food stalls would later emerge around these settlements.

The areas around Bangkok where these temporary urban villages can form have an incredible level of multilayeredness to them to begin with. For example, if you walk on the streets along the urban transportation systems, you will see the dazzling side of Bangkok that is lined with developments with American-style skyscrapers. However, if you ride the river ferries, you will instead get a feel of the old neighborhoods and of a cityscape made of informal shacks. The areas around the ferry stops are places of a public nature with markets, streetball courts, and open spaces, but all of these things, without exception, are built as assemblages of shack-like constructions made of polycarbonate panels and corrugated metal. If you step one street further into the depths of the residential areas off of the main streets, you will find dead-end streets everywhere around which relaxed neighborhoods that have a sense of common community have formed. These street communities stand right alongside each other, back-to-back.

Chat makes his architecture each time as though to enjoy Bangkok's multilayereness by employing an editorial approach. The idea of acceptance, a sense of fun, and editing are the engines that generate Chat's architecture. He is not interested in clearly recognizable authorship. What is most important to him before anything else is the act of observing the city that is to be accepted and enjoyed. When we visited his hotel project in an old neighborhood, Chat took the trouble of putting us on a ferry and of taking us on a walk around the old neighborhood across a variety of routes. It was only after we had traversed the different routes and had felt like we had grasped an understanding of how the neighborhood represented a fusion of the various changes over the years that he finally began explaining the architecture.

The dead-end streets and the thresholds between the street and architecture in Chat's architectural designs—which can be said to be more authentic/high-quality than not—are solidly backed by the idea of valuing the freedom and dignity of the residents by protecting their rights to the city and their activities in the street. The Thaibrids, which variously reflect the freedom for one to wander around in the city, a freedom from context, the freedom for one to use the street, and the freedom of editing, appear to be diversiform at first glance, but I have come to appreciate that they are all grounded in the architect's attitude of respect for the city's residents and for their right to freely move around and to freely lead their lives.

Far Afield from the Ocean Current

Each time we held another meeting on the road, I felt that we all needed to get together at some point. I wanted to avoid turning the exhibition into a simple showcase of emerging Asian architects. I needed to engage in deep dialogue with the exhibitors if I was going to make an exhibition that would respond to them in an organic way. E-mail and Skype sufficed when we worked with a set routine, but they were not suited for holding intensive discussions. Fortunately, TOTO had plans to host a big lecture by Sou FUJIMOTO in Singapore. I jumped on the opportunity to ask them to summon all parties and miraculously managed to get all five architects and the entire planning team to meet at once. Sou FUJIMOTO's lecture was titled "FUTURES OF THE FUTURE".

On the day after the lecture, the five architects, Mr. VIRAY, GALLERY·MA's planning team, and I met for the whole day to talk. It was difficult to settle on anything, but I had expected as much (talented architects are such difficult people!). Even though I could take charge of the exhibition's layout on my own responsibility, we wanted everyone to be in agreement on at least the exhibition's theme, so we pushed the discussion further. When we were finally all thoroughly exhausted, the exhibitors still were not settled on what direction they wanted to take, but they did have some consensus on where they did not want to go. Firstly, they did not want to use the word "future". Secondly, they did not want to use the word "new". I could not help myself from sharing a wry laugh with Mr. VIRAY at how much this contrasted with the lecture by Sou FUJIMOTO that we had heard the previous night. Mr. VIRAY proposed the phrase "the Asian everyday". While not everyone was in full agreement with it, nobody seemed to have anything to say against it because everyone was interested in the idea of the "everyday" and of "being natural". I was bothered by the term "Asian" though; my relentless whining led to the addition of the subtitle "in the shifting world". I felt that we could heighten the preciousness of "the everyday" by bringing into the picture a feeling of urgency that suggested a great crisis could be just around the corner.

Strangely enough, when I look back on the experience of visiting the five architects, I do not have the impression of their work being particularly "Asian". As you can see by plotting the architects on a map, the four non-Japanese architects are based neither too far from nor too close to Japan—and in fact, they actually line up nicely from Singapore to Dali along the north-south axis running through the Malay Peninsula. What could this mean? The four architects also happen to have personal ties to Japan, and they have definitely been influenced in their ideas by contemporary Japanese architects.

The impression I have is of a situation in which the diverse frame-based architectural cultures from along the Pacific Rim are responding to and mixing with the architectural cultures of the Eurasian continent that are based on solidity and plasticity. I am not certain whether this situation can be described as what ecologist/ethnologist Tadao Umesao spoke of as "civilizational succession", but it seems that contemporary architecture is wriggling about like slime mold taking new shape in the area around the edges of Eurasia and Oceania that is neither too far from nor too close to Europe or Japan. And this slime mold clearly has its roots in Japan. When we look back over toward Japan, we see peculiar shapeless architecture emerging. As we find ourselves at the back end of the temporal vacuum of a difficult age, the pressure is building on us by the day to make a decision: Do we jump into the current of succession, or do we instead deliberately "stand apart"? Which direction for architecture is more alluring to you?

TOTO GALLERY·MA 30th Anniversary Exhibition Space Design
Architect, Associate professor at Yokohama National University,
Y-GSA (Yokohama Graduate School of Architecture)

海流から遠く離れて

藤原徹平

なぜ「アジア」か？　Why Asia?

　TOTOギャラリー・間の30周年展をアジアの若手建築家5組のグループ展でやる、というアイデアを聞いた時に、正直なところなぜアジアという「地域」に限定するのか？という疑問が浮かんできた。5年前の25周年展は「グローバル・エンズ」というテーマで、グローバリズムが席巻する世界において「地域」という文脈では語りきれない「個」の建築の出現がレポートされていた。「個」の独特さが「地域」の枠組を越えて「世界」や「歴史」と創造的に応答していくという状況が示された5年後に、なぜ再びアジアにフォーカスする必要があるのだろうか？　ビライ氏とTOTOギャラリー・間の企画チームに問うと、東日本大震災のことが胸中にあるという返答が返ってきた。東日本大震災のあと、元気を失っている若手建築家や学生たちを勇気づけ、希望を与えるような展示にしたいということだった。少子高齢化、急激な人口減少、経済低迷、収入減少、雇用不安、社会保障不安、地域の崩壊など高次の社会リスクが併発する状況を最近は「ジャパン・シンドローム」と呼ぶらしいのだが、そこに数百年に1度という災害が重なった。あれから4年経つが、依然として日本の社会は緊迫している。希望を軽々しく語るわけにはいかないが、だからこそ希望が必要だという気持ちもよくわかる。

　「アジア」を扱うことでどのような希望を描けるだろうか。もし「アジアは高度経済成長中だから」というような目線で希望を与えようというのだとすれば、その発想自体に私は希望を感じない。経済が良好だから「建築」が建つわけでなく、むしろマーケットの力の過剰さは「建築」の成り立ちを単純化する。

　私たちは、今、困難な時代に生きている。世界中で頻発する巨大な災害、金融危機などの甚大な社会的「危機」、こうした個人の力では抵抗しがたい巨大な出来事が、日常のすぐ横に在る。私が本展に期待をしたいのは、アジアの思想、宗教、風土が、この困難な時代に生み出そうとする＜文明論的な＞建築の行方であり、人間的な応答だ。困難な時代を乗り越えていく希望、その希望と共に在る「建築」とはいかなるものだろうか。

シンガポール　／　リン・ハオ
人工都市に織り込まれた、生命的身体の空間

　空港に降り立ち2月なのにすごく暑いのに驚く。それもそのはずで、機内で世界地図

をみたらほとんど赤道直下だ。リー・クワン・ユーが絶望から涙を見せたという望まざる独立宣言から50年。60の小さな島からなるシンガポールの今日の成功は、過激と形容してもよい実験的都市政策・経済政策の賜物である。

シンガポール滞在の宿はリトル・インディアという下町エリアにとった。リトル・インディアは、マレーシアでは5 foot way、台湾では騎廊などと呼ばれるショップハウスのつくる楽しい街で、勝手な先入観から超高層ビルが乱立するシティスケープを想像していたので、良質な「都市組織（アーバン・ティッシュ）」の存在に驚く。

カンフーの師範が近所にふらりと、というような独特の風貌とリラックスした空気をまとってリン・ハオがホテルにやってきた。リン・ハオは国籍こそマレーシア人だが、シンガポールとシドニーで建築を学び、現在はシンガポールで働いている。聞けば、今はスタッフを雇わず事務所スペースももたず、マックブックプロを片手に遊牧民のようにふらふらしながら設計しているという自由さだ。結構大きなプロジェクトもデザインしているので、どうやっているのか聞いてみると少し大きなプロジェクトの場合は大学時代の友人の建築家カップルと協働しているようだ。ホテルのカフェで、プロジェクトのプレゼンテーションを受けた後に、自主製本した文庫サイズの作品集を手渡された。実に味のあるモノクロームのCADドローイング中心の作品集だった。ものすごくハイセンスな感性とイージーゴーイングでリラックスした身体性とが同居している。

翌日見たリン・ハオの建築は本人と同じくらいインパクトがあった。一番印象に残っているのが彼の建築の中を流れる風だ。どこにいてもゆったりと微風が流れている。一方、空間のスケールは、大胆。人間の身体というよりも、もっと大きな尺度、ランドスケープ的と言っても良いおおらかな空間に包まれる。

リン・ハオは、下町のリトル・インディアを推薦するだけあって「都市」への愛着が深い。プロジェクトの説明も、いつも決まって敷地の「都市組織」の成り立ちから解説してくれる。彼の空間は新しい感性にあふれているが、建築思想としては本格派。シンガポールはジャ

ングルですら人工的に生成してしまうような人工的な都市国家である。リン・ハオはその人工性を完璧に理解しつつも、その人工的な環境を有機的に解釈し、生物的な建築の応答を試みる。「都市組織」の中に織り込まれた生命的な空間の存在に心が大きく動かされる。

大理　／　チャオ・ヤン
「離れて」「立つ」建築の共振

　シンガポールから深夜フライトで上海に飛び、そのまま大理まで中国の国内線に乗り継ぐ。赤道直下の群島から一気にチベットに連なる連峰まで移動すると、さすがに地球の大きさを感じる。季節も夏から冬へ逆戻りだ。大理は、大理石の産地として名高く、ミャンマーやチベットとの交易で古くから栄えた都市だ。

　私たちはてっきりチャオ・ヤンが大理の出身なのかと思っていたが、旅で訪れ気に入って移住をしたのだという（ちなみに彼は重慶の出身）。確かに、雄大な蒼山連峰を背に湖をのぞむ環境は神話の舞台のようであり、大理石で築かれた旧市街も美しい。にしてもなんという決断の軽やかさだろうか。調べてみると大理はバックパッカーが長期滞在してしまう「沈没地」として知られ、国内外からの移住者が多いらしい。それは大理が少数民族の白族の住む地域であることと関係があるようだ。少数民族の尊重ということで、中央政府からの政治的な介入が穏やかで、古くから続くユーラシア大陸の交易都市の多言語・多文化の社会が存続している場所ということだろうか。

　自分は大理にとって歴史上最初の「建築家」なはずです、とヤンは笑いながら話す。設計料が何かということから説明が必要な辺境の地に家族で居を構え、事務所をつくったのには、美しさや多文化の交差点ということと同時に大工や職人などの文化の存在も大きいようだ。職人とじっくりと話し合いながら建築をつくっていける状況そのものが中国では得難いことであり、それに加えて北京や上海といった巨大都市圏から離れることで経済的なスピードや行き過ぎた効率性の要求から距離をとるという深慮もありそうだ。あえて「離れて」「立つ」という創造的な態度がそこにある。

　ところでヤンの建築は文字通りに「離れて」「立つ」建築が多い。雄大な自然の中にポツンと建つ建築にふさわしく、シンプルで強い形、そして美しいプロポーションをしている。比例や形の問題だけでなく、量塊（ソリッド）と空隙（ボイド）、と架構（フレーム）が応答し合うことによって生じる化学反応によって、周囲と力強く響き合う。

　チャオ・ヤンの建設中のプロジェクトを見に、湖の小島へと船で渡る。島にあるふたつのプロジェクトはいずれもホテルで、島の路地が不便なため舟に乗ってホテルにアクセスをすることになるという。「離れて」「立つ」建築だからこそ、建築を訪れる道行も建築休

験の一部にしていこうという意欲、庭園的な空間の組み立てを取り入れようという意識を強く感じる。これはかつて杭州の建築家のワン・シューからも強烈に感じたことだが、「庭園」ということは日本と中国の間に横たわる重要な空間思想ということなのだろう。

　漁村の路地を歩いていると、ふとチャオ・ヤンが街角にそびえる住宅の外壁を指し示し、この壁が私の建築の先生だと紹介してくれた。その壁は、表情の違う石積みの層が４層、土壁の層が３層、漆喰仕上げの層が２層、その上に木組みの架構と瓦屋根と、合計すれば10層くらいの、お菓子のミルフィーユのような立面をしている独特のもので、チャオ・ヤンは、地元の大工からこの壁の層の意味をひとつひとつ教わったのだという。機能性ということだけでは説明しきれない、人類史の精神が建築で描かれたようなすごみのある壁だった。「離れて」「立つ」ことでこんなものに出合ってしまうものなのか。

ホーチミン　／　ヴォ・チョン・ギア
建築の向きあう正面

　ギアの建築の「核」には間違いなく初期から試みられ続けている一連の竹の建築がある。竹独特の構法やディテール、形の面白さというのもあるし、竹建築を施工する職人集団から企画・組織してしまうギアのプロデューサーとしての能力の高さも余すことなく説明する。ギアは日本で内藤廣の下で建築を学ぶが、小嶋一浩らと共同設計していたホーチミン大学のプロジェクトからの影響も感じるし、安藤忠雄のメッセージ性の強さも意識している節がある。日本建築家のロールモデルへのどん欲な関心や知的好奇心の幅の広さ、抜群の行動力から考えれば、彼がすでにホーチミンとハノイの２都市に事務所を構え、数十人のスタッフを抱えているというサクセス・ストーリーにも得心がいく。

　私がそんなギアのたくさんの才能の引出しから取り上げたいのは、「House for Tree」という一連の住宅プロジェクトについてだ。ギアは建築家がオーダーメードで住宅をつくるということ自体に対してかなり批判的な態度をとっている。住宅の設計から始めることの多い日本の若手建築家には耳が痛いところだ。ギアは日本から多くのことを学んでいるが、同時に日本への批判精神の眼差しもするどい。

　彼が投げ掛けるのは、歯止めのきかないスプロール化、人工物で埋め尽くされる都市をどうするのか？という根本的な問い掛けだ。そこで彼が選んだのは、住宅を住宅としてつくるのではなく、都市に自然を取り戻すための機会としてとらえるという発想だ。House「for」Tree。建築の向き合う先（for）にあるのは何か。本質だけをシンプルに問おうという姿勢は、力強い。ギアがもし本当に今後住宅を「House for Tree」のコンセプトでつくり続ければ、本当にベトナムの都市に森が出現するかもしれない。

ホーチミン滞在中に、「藤原さんもメディテーションやった方がいいよ」と何度も勧誘されたのだが、実際ギアの事務所では朝と夕方にメディテーションの時間がある。ブッダが悟りを開いたメソッドを取り入れたメディテーションなのだという。何十もの仕事を抱える忙しい身だからこそ、外部を遮断して瞑想し精神集中することで、むしろ創造的になるとギアは言う。日本が文化として失いつつある一番重要なものはメディテーションの伝統だと、またもドキリとすることを言う。ギアは間違いなくベトナムを代表する第一人者の建築家として紹介すべき人物である。すでに大所帯の事務所であるし、多数の成功は彼の思想をぼやかすが、私は建築の行方の先「for」を問い掛けるギアのラディカルな態度に、困難な時代の建築への希望を強く感じる。

東京　／　大西麻貴＋百田有希
「人間のなりわい」と建築

　大西麻貴と百田有希の事務所は東京の下町の街角にある。まるで印刷工場や豆腐屋のように、目一杯道に開放され、建具もない吹きさらしの場所だ（冬は一応ビニールカーテンがある）。この事務所に移ってから彼らの建築が少し変わってきているように思う。もともと学生時代から活動をしている建築家ユニットだから、常識にとらわれない自由さというものがあったが、経験を積んで大人になるというよりもむしろ「常識にとらわれない」というあたりが本格的になってきている。時に建築じゃないようなことも平気でする。

　何が彼らの主題なのかと観察してみると、建築に限らず、「人間のなりわい」ということ全体に興味があるようだ。「人間のなりわい」から考えるという姿勢は、彼らに限らず日本の若手建築家や学生に広くみられる傾向だ。（それは日本の外側から見ると、アトリエ・ワンの子供たちということになるのだろうか）。しかし、実際のところ「人間のなりわい」と建築の関係を考えるのは魅力的だが容易なことではない。なにしろ「なりわい」は不定形（アモルフ）でとらえどころがない。しかも大西と百田は、アトリエ・ワンのように建築タイポロジー分析を用いず、むしろ避けるようにして遊戯的実験的に進めている。ある時は例えば「人間のなりわい」を不思議な形をした容器のような建築に閉じ込めてみたり、「人間のなりわい」の宿り木になるような＜場＞を散在させてみたり、時には不思議な「人間のなりわい」を生み出す装置そのものを考えたりする。また、彼らは本や展覧会や演劇といった他のメディアにも興味があるようだ。考えてみたら、本や展覧会や演劇も不定形の「人間のなりわい」を閉じ込めて、形や名前を与えていくものだから当然なことかもしれない。

　彼らが向かう先に何が見えているのだろうか。私は、彼らがやりたいことは「閉じない物語」と呼ぶべきものではないかと考えている。良かれ悪しかれ「物語」は必ず閉じるもの

だ。一方「建築の経験」というのは、本来はどこからどこまでが建築なのか区切りようがない。彼らは、経験が閉じない建築というジャンルを利用して「閉じない物語」ということをつくろうとしているのではないか。それゆえに必要以上に物語を建築の形式に閉じ込めてしまうタイポロジー的な発想を退けるのではないかということを勝手に外野から想像している。それはもしかすると、非建築を建築するというようなユニークな態度であるかもしれない。ふたりを切り込み隊長に、アメーバや粘菌のような形のない建築、「閉じない物語」を生み出そうという現代日本の建築錬金術の行方には個人的に大変興味がそそられる。

バンコク ／ チャトポン・チュエンルディーモル
「タイブリッド」と生命的身体の都市

　チャットはいまどき珍しく事務所のホームページすら開設していない。そのため、彼の情報がなかなか手に入らなくて、最初に見付けたのはFacebookにアップされていた彼の自邸と、バンコクのバラックのリサーチだった。バラックのリサーチの中には、チャットが設計した建築では？　と誤解させるほどの強度のある空間が現れていて、そのリサーチの写真だけで彼の能力を信頼させる迫力があった。

　タイという国はなんでも受け入れちゃうからなあと、タイのことをよく知る友人が愛着をもってよく言うのだが、実際にバンコクに来てみると確かにいろんな文化が混ざり合っている。アメリカ的なショッピングモール、日本式のデパート、コンビニエンスストア。

　タイらしさ？　タイらしさなんてないよ。なんでも受け入れて混ざり合って融合する（Hybrid）のがタイらしさだよ。といつも陽気なチャットはそう話している最中に「Thaibrid（タイブリッド）」という言葉を発明してしまった。彼の奥さんがリサーチしているというタイの農村で作られる竹細工の素晴らしさの村ごとの違いについて熱心に言及したかと思うと、でもタイらしさなんてないよとあっけらかんとしていて、ジャック・タチの映画が大好きだとポスターを紹介してくれる。

私たちが強く関心をもったバラックは、バンコクの大きな建設現場にできるワーカーのための現場小屋、「都市の中のインフォーマルでテンポラリーな村」なのだということが分かった。バンコクの現場のワーカーはほとんど海外や郊外からの出稼ぎだ。大きい現場ならば団地のような現場小屋ムラが出来る。現場小屋ムラの周りには、日用品を売るマーケットが建ち、屋台が出来る。

　このように都市の中にテンポラリーな村が出来てしまう、バンコクの界隈の多重性はそもそも半端ない。例えば、都市交通システムに沿って街を歩くとアメリカ式の超高層ビル開発プロジェクトが並ぶ煌びやかなバンコクが見えてくるが、水上バスに乗ってみるとむしろ旧市街の気配やインフォーマルなバラックの街並みを感じる。水上バスの降り場の周りは、マーケットやらストリートバスケのコートやら広場といったパブリックな場だが、それらは例外なくポリカーボネート板やトタンの波板でつぎはぎされたバラック的な建築群である。またメインストリートから1本住宅街の奥に足を踏み入れると、行き止まりの路地だらけで、路地を中心として落ち着いた界隈、コモンが形成されている。こうした界隈が背中合わせに近接していく。

　チャットの建築はそうしたバンコクの多重性を楽しむように、その都度、編集的につくられる。「受容」と「楽しさ」と「編集」。これがチャットの建築を創造するエンジンだ。ひと目でわかる作家性にはむしろ興味がない。まず肝心なのは受け入れて楽しむべき「都市への観察」ということになる。旧市街のホテルのプロジェクトを訪ねた時には、チャットはまずわれわれをわざわざ水上バスに乗せ、旧市街の中をさまざまなルートで連れ歩いた。いろいろなルートを巡り、時代の変化を受容しながら融合する地域の様子を理解できたなという頃合いに、ようやく建築の説明が始まる。

　行き止まりの街路、街路と建築の境界、どちらかというとオーセンティックで上質なチャットの建築デザインの裏側には、都市への権利、路上のアクティビティという生活者の自由や尊厳を大切にしようという思想がどっしりとある。都市をさまよう自由、コンテクストからの自由、路上を使う自由、編集の自由、一見多様に見えるタイプリッドには、移動と自由、生活と自由というような都市生活者を尊重する建築家の態度があるのだと思った。

海流から遠く離れて

　旅先で打合せをするたび、一度全員で会う必要を感じていた。アジアの新人建築家のショーケースになることは避けたい。有機的に応答する展示にするには、密度の濃い対話が必要だ。電子メールやSkypeでは、決められたルーチンは進められるが濃い議論するのには不向きだ。幸いなことに、シンガポールでTOTO主催の藤本壮介の大規模なレ

クチャーが開かれるという。それに便乗するかたちで全員に集合を呼び掛けてもらったところ、奇跡的に5組の建築家と企画チーム全員集まれることになった。藤本壮介のレクチャータイトルは「未来の未来」。

　レクチャーの翌日、5組の建築家とビライ氏、ギャラリー・間の企画チームでまる1日議論を重ねる。予想はしていたが、全然まとまらない（有能な建築家たちというのはなんと厄介な連中なのか！）。会場構成は私のほうで責任をもって引き取れるが、展覧会テーマだけはどうにか全員で合意したいので、さらに議論を重ねていく。みなヘトヘトになったころ、向かいたい先はまとまらないものの、向かいたくない先は輪郭を現してきた。

　まずひとつ。「未来」という言葉は使いたくない

　もうひとつ。「新しい」という言葉も使いたくない

　昨晩聞いた藤本壮介のレクチャーとのコントラストがすごいので思わずビライ氏と苦笑。「アジアの日常」という語はビライ氏からの提案。全員、大賛成ということではないものの、「日常」「自然体」ということに興味はあるから異論はないという様子。アジアという語にひっかかる私がごねまくって、「in the shifting world（移りゆく世界において）」という副題がくっついた。重大な危機がすぐ横にあるという緊迫感を共有することで、「日常」ということの尊さが生きてくるはずだ。

　ところで5組の建築家を訪ねた経験を振り返ってみると、不思議と「アジア」という印象がない。そもそも地図にプロットしてみるとよくわかるが、日本以外の4組は、日本からほどよく距離が離れていて、しかもシンガポールから大理というようにマレー半島の南北軸に沿って綺麗に並んでいく。これはどういうことだろうか。しかも、4組の建築家とも日本との個別の縁や現代の日本人建築家からの思想的な影響がある。

　私が感じたのは、日本の現代建築をひとつの母系にして、環太平洋的に広がる多様な「架構」の建築文化、ユーラシア大陸の「量塊で彫塑的」な建築文化、が応答し交じり合っていくような状況だ。この状況が、かつて梅棹忠夫が述べたような＜文明の遷移（サクセッション）＞ということであるかは分からないが、日本からも欧州からもほどよく距離が離れたユーラシア・オセアニアの縁において、現代建築が粘菌のようにうごめいて変容しつつある。そしてこの粘菌のルーツは明らかに日本にある。日本を振り返ると、なにやら不思議な形にならない建築が生まれている。困難な時代のぽっかりと空いた時間の裏側で、決断を迫る圧力は日に日に強まっている。遷移の海流に飛び込むのか、むしろあえて「離れて」「立つ」のか。あなたを惹きつける＜建築の行方＞はどこにあるのか。

TOTOギャラリー・間30周年記念展　会場デザイン
建築家、横浜国立大学大学院Y-GSA准教授

Credits
クレジット

English translation | 英訳

Gen Machida | マチダ・ゲン
p. 17, p. 51, p. 85, p. 119, p. 153, pp. 188-196

Japanese translation | 和訳

Moriyuki Ogawa | 小川守之
pp. 10-13, pp. 19-49, p. 53, p. 55, pp. 57-62,
pp. 64-67, pp. 69-71, pp. 73-77, p. 79, pp. 81-82,
p. 87, p. 121, p. 155, p. 156, pp. 158-159,
pp. 161-166, pp. 168-169, pp. 171-178, pp. 181-184

Drawings | 図版提供

Chaiyasat Settasagulchai
p. 22, p. 25, p. 26

Ploypailin Puttipongpokai, Silapakorn University
p. 24

Rung-arun Tiyanukulmongkhon
p. 33

Surada Sangwornchart, Silapakorn University
p. 38

Rerngsiri Tanasiripong
p. 40 (middle), p. 49

Supaporn Neumtatian, Rangsit University
p. 40 (bottom)

Karn Chuensawang, Rangsit University
p. 41 (bottom left)

Thanyawarat Tuonti, Rangsit University
p. 41 (bottom middle)

Kornkanok Nurat, Rangsit University
p. 41 (bottom right)

Pitchaya Poonsin, Manita Bavornkiratikajorn, Sukumal Yuktananda
p. 46

Tanarat Prachaanuwong, Chulalongkorn University
p. 48

Photographs | 写真提供

Pirak Anurakyawachon, Spaceshift Studio
pp. 22-23 (top), p. 29 (top)

Room Magazine
p. 25, p. 27 (top), p. 28 (top)

Ketsiree Wongwan
pp. 30-31 (top), p. 33, p. 34 (middle), p. 35 (top),
pp. 36-37 (top), p. 39 (top), p. 40 (top),
pp. 42-43 (top), p. 45, p. 47 (top), p. 48, p. 49 (top)

Barry Broman
p. 46

Beton Brut
pp. 56-57, p. 58 (left), p. 72 (top), pp. 73-74,
p. 75 (top, bottom right)

Koo
p.58 (right)

Fabian Ong
p. 59 (middle, bottom), p. 70

Jeremy San
pp. 61-63, p. 65, p. 71 (top), pp. 76-83

Jovian Lim
p. 66-67

Tan Hai Han
p. 71 (bottom right)

Hiroyuki Oki
pp. 92-93, p. 94 (bottom), pp. 96-99, pp. 104-115,
p. 116 (top right, bottom), p. 117 (top, bottom right)

Phan Quang
p. 94 (top), p. 95

PHOTOGRAPHERS4EXPO – Saverio Lombardi Vallauri
pp. 100-101

Kai Nakamura | 中村 絵
pp. 124-149 (background), p. 127 (bottom right)

Zhinong Xi
pp. 156-157

Jonathan Leijonhufvud
p. 158

Su Chen
p. 162 (bottom)

※ All other images/drawings provided by the architects.
上記以外は 各建築設計事務所より提供。

監修 | エルウィン・ビライ

建築評論家。1961年フィリピン生まれ。1982年フィリピン大学建築学部卒業。1986年京都工芸繊維大学大学院工芸学研究科建築学専攻修士課程終了。1991年東京大学大学院工学研究科建築学専攻博士課程修了。シンガポール国立大学デザイン環境学部建築学専攻准教授を務めた後、2011年7月より京都工芸繊維大学工芸科学研究科建築造形学部門教授。2015年6月に同大学特任教授、学長補佐官に就任。

Editorial Supervision | Erwin VIRAY

Architectural critic. Born in 1961. Graduated from the University of Philippines College of Architecture in 1982. Completed the master's program of the Department of Architecture in the Kyoto Institute of Technology Graduate School of Science and Technology in 1986. Completed the doctoral program of the Department of Architecture in the University of Tokyo Graduate School of Engineering in 1991. Taught as an associate professor at the Department of Architecture in the National University of Singapore School of Design & Environment before becoming a professor of the Department of Design and Architecture in the Kyoto Institute of Technology School of Science and Technology in July 2011. Global Excellence Professor and University President Aide since June 2015.

アジアの日常から —— 変容する世界での可能性を求めて

2015年10月16日　初版第1刷発行

編集：TOTO出版
監修：エルウィン・ビライ
著者：チャトポン・チュエンルディーモル、リン・ハオ、ヴォ・チョン・ギア、
　　　大西麻貴＋百田有希、チャオ・ヤン

発行者：加藤 徹
発行所：TOTO出版（TOTO株式会社）
　　　　〒107-0062 東京都港区南青山1-24-3
　　　　TOTO乃木坂ビル2F
　　　　［営業］TEL: 03-3402-7138　FAX: 03-3402-7187
　　　　［編集］TEL: 03-3497-1010
　　　　　　　URL: http://www.toto.co.jp/publishing/
デザイン：色部義昭、本間洋史（株式会社日本デザインセンター 色部デザイン研究室）
印刷・製本：図書印刷株式会社

落丁本・乱丁本はお取り替えいたします。本書の全部又は一部に対するコピー・スキャン・デジタル化等の無断複製行為は、著作権法上での例外を除き禁じます。本書を代行業者等の第三者に依頼してスキャンやデジタル化することは、たとえ個人や家庭内での利用であっても著作権上認められておりません。
定価はカバーに表示してあります。

©2015 Erwin Viray, Chatpong Chuenrudeemol, Ling Hao, Vo Trong Nghia,
Maki Onishi+Yuki Hyakuda, Yang Zhao, TOTO Publishing
Printed in Japan
ISBN978-4-88706-354-9

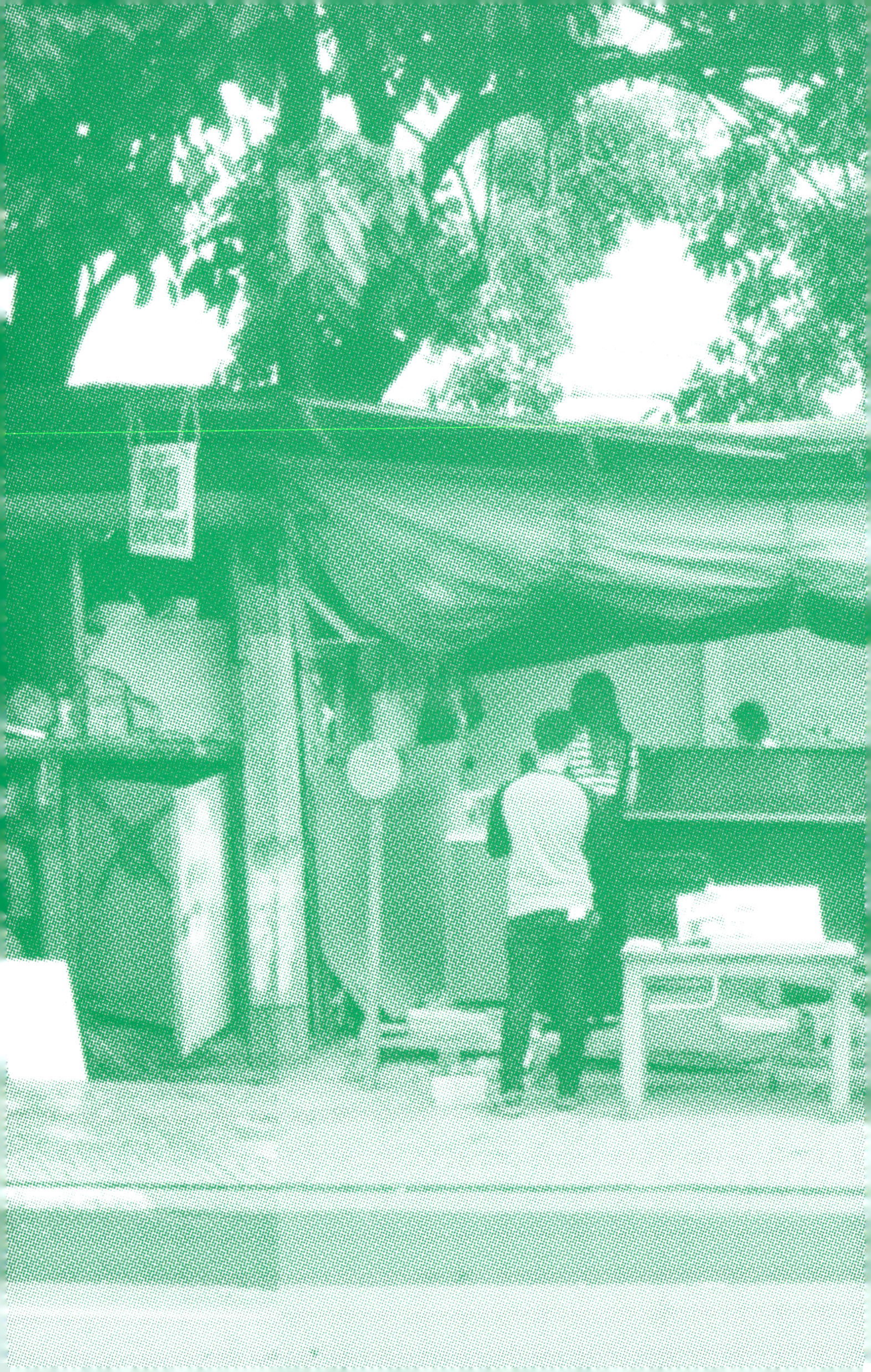